HANK
AARON

Baseball Player

Michael Benson

Ferguson
An imprint of ☑️ Facts On File

Hank Aaron: Baseball Player

Ferguson
An imprint of Facts On File, Inc.
132 West 31st Street
New York NY 10001

Library of Congress Cataloging-in-Publication Data
Benson, Michael.
    Hank Aaron, baseball player / Michael Benson.
        p. cm
    Includes index.
    ISBN 0-8160-5349-9 (hc : alk. paper)
    1. Aaron, Hank, 1934—Juvenile literature. 2. Baseball players—United States—Biography—Juvenile literature. I. Title.
    GV865.A25B46 2004
    796.357′092—dc22   2004001745

Ferguson books are available at special discounts when purchased in bulk quantities for businesses, associations, institutions, or sales promotions. Please call our Special Sales Department in New York at (212) 967-8800 or (800) 322-8755.

You can find Ferguson on the World Wide Web at http://www.fergpubco.com

Text design by David Strelecky

Pages 96–112 adapted from *Ferguson's Encyclopedia of Careers and Vocational Guidance, Twelfth Edition*

Printed in the United States of America

MP Hermitage 10 9 8 7 6 5 4 3 2 1

This book is printed on acid-free paper.

CONTENTS

1

A RECORD NUMBER OF RECORDS

Although Henry "Hank" Aaron is best known as the man who broke Babe Ruth's record for most career home runs, this is hardly his only baseball achievement. Among his other most notable records are most home runs with one club (Braves, 733), RBIs, or runs batted in (2,297), total bases (6,856 [that's the number of bases a batter has gained through his hits, i.e., a single is worth one base, a double worth two bases, a triple worth three, and a home run worth four]), and most games played (3,298).

Hank hit 20 or more home runs for 20 straight seasons. He hit more than 40 home runs a season in eight seasons. He played in 24 All-Star games, which ties the record held by baseball greats Willie Mays and Stan Musial. Hank won the Gold Glove Award for excellence in playing the outfield three times, in 1958, 1959, and 1960. He was named *The Sporting News*'s National League Player of the Year in 1956 and 1963.

Hank was chosen the National League Most Valuable Player (MVP) in 1957 and finished in the top 10 in MVP voting 12 other times. He led the National League in hitting (batting average) in 1956 and 1959. He led the league four times in slugging average, in 1959, 1963, 1967, and 1971. He also led the league four times in home runs, in 1957, 1963, 1966, and 1967, and four times in RBIs, in 1957, 1960, 1963, and 1966. He was inducted into the Baseball Hall of Fame in Cooperstown, New York, in 1982.

But Hank Aaron will always be remembered as more than just a skilled ballplayer. He was also a man who broke through the color line—social barriers that held back African Americans. He is a champion of civil rights, a man who has been outspoken on racial issues for most of his adult life.

When Jackie Robinson broke the color line in 1947 by becoming the first African American in the 20th century to play Major League Baseball, black athletes were not instantly treated the same as their white teammates. Gaining equality was a slow process.

Things have improved since that time thanks to men like Hank who dared to call attention to the problem. But racial unfairness still exists today, both on and off the

Hank Aaron will always be remembered as both a record-setting baseball player and a civil rights champion. (National Baseball Hall of Fame Library, Cooperstown, NY)

baseball playing field. Hank continues to point this out every chance he gets.

Hank's mom wanted him to go to college to become a teacher, so that he could make a difference in the world. But by following his dreams of a career in baseball, Hank Aaron has been able to make a world of difference in his own way.

2

DOWN THE BAY

Henry Louis Aaron was born February 5, 1934, in the "Down the Bay" section of Mobile, Alabama, which is on the Gulf of Mexico. The following day the most famous baseball player in the world, Babe Ruth of the New York Yankees, turned 39 years old. Forty years later Henry and "the Babe's" names would be forever linked.

When Hank was a baby, his father, Herbert, worked on the docks, loading and unloading ships. His mother, Estella, stayed home with the children. Six years before Hank was born, Herbert climbed a tree outside Hartwell Field in Mobile where the New York Yankees were playing an exhibition game. That day, the Babe hit a home run that landed in a coal car on a train that was passing by, headed for New Orleans.

Mobile, like much of the southern United States, was a place of great racial tension. African Americans did not

Babe Ruth, 1942 (Associated Press)

enjoy many of the basic freedoms that white people did, and many white people tried very hard to keep things that way. This situation frequently led to violence. For example, when Hank was eight there were riots at the docks of Mobile. White workers became violent when black workers were promoted instead of whites. Guards had to be hired to escort black workers, like Herbert Aaron, to and from work.

An Early Love of the Game

As a child, Hank had two great loves: baseball and Boy Scouts. Hank's mother always wished that he would work as hard at school as he worked at scouting.

Hank played ball a bit differently than most people. For example, he learned to hit a baseball in a most unusual way. Although he did everything right-handed, including swing a bat, he gripped the bat with his left hand above his right. This is called cross-handed batting. He continued to bat this way even during the early days of his pro career.

Most home run hitters keep their weight back as they begin their swing and rock onto their front foot to give the bat extra power. Hank did not do it that way. "I had my weight on my front foot, and I got my power from lashing out at the last second with my hands," he said.

The boys in Hank's neighborhood could not afford real baseball bats and balls, so they used whatever they could find or make to play the game. Ax or broom handles made good baseball bats. The children tied discarded nylon stockings around old golf balls to make a baseball. Or, if no golf ball was available, they tied rags into a clump. Even crumpled-up tin cans were used as baseballs. (Hank still bears a scar on his face where he was cut by a tin can that his brother Herbert had batted at him.)

One of Hank's major inspirations was baseball player Jackie Robinson, who first played Major League Baseball, breaking the color line, when Hank was 13 years old. Robinson, along with Joe Louis, another African American who was then the heavyweight boxing champion of the world, were the heroes in Hank's neighborhood.

The year after Robinson broke the color line, he traveled to Mobile to give an inspirational speech to the city's youth. Sitting in the audience was Hank. Jackie spoke of following your dreams, no matter how unlikely they may seem. It was while listening to Robinson speak that Aaron decided he was going to be a big-league ballplayer one day.

Jackie Robinson was one of Hank's major inspirations. (Associated Press)

The Negro Leagues

When Hank was a kid, white and black baseball players hardly ever played together. Black men were not allowed to play on white teams. One of the men responsible for keeping blacks from playing Major League Baseball was Adrian Constantine "Cap"

Anson, who played in the big leagues for 27 seasons. Starting in 1883, he refused to play in games in which blacks were playing. Four years later he persuaded the team owners to bar blacks from organized baseball.

During the years that African American ballplayers were not allowed to play in the majors, they formed their own leagues: the Negro Leagues. Many of the greatest ballplayers of all time played in the Negro Leagues. These included Hall of Famers such as James Thomas "Cool Papa" Bell and Josh Gibson. The Negro Leagues' biggest star pitcher was Satchel Paige, who, like Aaron, was from Mobile.

Integration, a policy that enforced equal opportunities for all races, put an end to the Negro Leagues. After Jackie Robinson began playing with the Brooklyn Dodgers, black fans stopped supporting the all-black teams. The first black stars to play alongside white players were veterans of the Negro Leagues—players such as Willie Mays, Luke Easter, and Roy Campanella. The all-black leagues struggled on for a few years, but by the early 1960s the Negro Leagues were out of business.

A New Home

In 1942 Herbert Aaron bought two plots of overgrown land in Toulminville, Alabama. He paid $55 apiece for them. He then paid a pair of carpenters $50 each and, using scraps of wood and other materials that he found lying around, they built a six-room house on those plots. Herbert, Estella, and the six Aaron children moved into the new house, which had no windows, no lights, and no running water. (There had been seven Aaron children, but one of Hank's younger brothers, Alfred, died of pneumonia at age two.)

There was an outhouse behind the big house that served as the bathroom, and the Aarons used a kerosene lamp for light. After Hank had made money playing baseball, an addition was built onto the house, and plumbing and electricity were added. But Hank's parents never moved out.

To make extra money, Herbert Aaron ran a bar called the Black Cat Inn next to the new house. When Hank was old enough, he helped contribute money to the family by picking potatoes, mowing lawns, and delivering ice (these were the days before refrigerators).

If Hank had not been able to make a living as a ballplayer, he would have sought a career as a carpenter. Hank's uncle, Bubba, was quite a ballplayer himself and taught Hank how to play.

In 1945 Toulminville officially became a part of Mobile, and the city built baseball fields right across the street from the Aaron house. "It was like having Ebbets Field [the old ballpark in Brooklyn, New York, where Jackie Robinson played] in my backyard," Hank later said.

A teenage Hank first played organized ball in a softball league run by the city recreation department. His team was called the Braves (a team name that would be prominent in Hank's career). He played catcher, pitcher, and infielder. He hit quite a few home runs. His nickname on the team was "Snowshoes," because he ran on his heels.

Trouble with School

As a kid, Hank was never a dedicated student, but he showed up and tried his best. However, after he decided to become a professional baseball player, things at school went downhill. All he thought about was baseball. "School didn't matter to me," Hank said.

Baseball was not the only sport that Hank was good at. He was a lineman on his high school football team, and a very good one. He was so good that he was offered a college scholarship to play football. This offer thrilled Hank's mother, who would have loved for him to go to college. But Hank turned the offer down. Baseball was his true love. He was afraid that he would get hurt playing football and miss his chance to play baseball for a living.

Soon after turning down the scholarship, he quit his high school football team. This angered his principal so much that he chased Hank down the hall waving a cane at him. The following spring Hank began to skip school so that he could listen to baseball games on the radio and shoot pool at the local billiard hall. After missing more than a month of school, he was caught and expelled for truancy.

When Hank was expelled, his father gave him a lecture, explaining how much he had sacrificed for Hank. He said that he had given Hank more food money than he had taken for himself, because he knew it would be impossible for his son to learn on an empty stomach. Herbert told his son that he did not mind him playing baseball—he understood Hank's dreams and wanted him to make a living on the baseball diamond one day—but he told Hank that he had to go to school first. Hank's mother did not want her son to be a ballplayer, but she also insisted that he return to school so that he could one day become a teacher.

Heeding his parents' advice, Hank did return to school after he was expelled, but he never graduated. Eventually he chose baseball over school, and he stood by his decision.

Getting Noticed

In 1951 while Hank was playing softball for the Braves, a man named Ed Scott, who was a scout for a local semipro team, approached him. (A scout watches many ballgames in the hopes of finding someone talented enough to play for the team he or she represents.) Scott knew he had a solid candidate in Hank Aaron.

Scott told Aaron that his team, the Mobile Black Bears, played on Sunday afternoons and the pay was $10 a game. Hank was thrilled to learn that, if he played, he would get a uniform. But Hank said he would have to ask his mom.

Hank's mother said okay, but he could only play the home games. That way he would still be able to attend church every Sunday.

As an adult, Aaron stands 6 feet tall and weighs 190 pounds, not exceptionally large for a big-league ballplayer. But at 17, he was not even that big. When his new teammates first saw him, they had their doubts that he would be able to play. He appeared to be a boy playing among men. But it did not take long for them to change their minds. At Hank's first batting practice it was clear that he could hit the ball a mile.

While playing for the semipro team, another scout noticed Hank. His name was Bunny Downs, and he recruited talent for the Indianapolis Clowns of the Negro American League.

When Downs approached Hank, Hank told him that he was underage and that his mom wanted him to finish school. Downs told Hank that he would be back to talk when Hank turned 18. Hank assumed the man would forget about him by that time.

But Downs did not forget. Days after Hank turned 18, while he was only halfway through his senior year of high school, a contract from the Clowns arrived. The contract offered $200 per month. Hank promised his mother and father that he would finish school later and signed the contract. A few days later he was told to report to spring training in Winston-Salem, North Carolina.

On His Way

In 1952 Hank Aaron left the state of Alabama for the first time. Carrying a sack filled with sandwiches his mother had made, and wearing a pair of pants he had borrowed from his sister Sarah, he headed for Winston-Salem, North Carolina, where the Clowns held their spring training. (Although the team was still known as the Indianapolis Clowns, they had not played a game in Indianapolis in many years. They barnstormed, which means they moved from town to town without ever really playing a game in their home city.)

Hank's teammates gave him a chilly reception. The team's reaction was nothing personal, however, it was just business. From their perspective, every new guy that made the team put a veteran player out of a job.

While he was with the Clowns Hank experienced racism firsthand. He had known that African Americans were treated as second-class citizens during his youth in Mobile, but now he got to see just how ugly racism could be. Because restaurants and hotels would not serve the Clowns, they were forced to eat and sleep on the bus.

During his first month with the Clowns, Hank hit over .400. That means that he hit more than four hits for every 10 times he came to bat (walks do not count). The Clowns' owner, Syd Pollack, was very impressed with Hank's play. Fans quickly heard about Hank's hitting ability and showed up at the ballpark to see him. Hank was what was called a "drawing card": He drew fans with his bat. The Clowns even had posters made up with Hank's picture on them.

Pollack made money from his team in two ways. For one, he sold tickets to the games. Second, he sold his ballplayers' contracts to the big leagues and their farm teams. Pollack contacted John Mullen, who was the head scout for the Boston Braves of the National League, and said he had a young ballplayer Mullen ought to take a look at.

Mullen sent a scout named Dewey Griggs to see Hank play. The Clowns were playing a game in Buffalo, New York, when Griggs arrived. He watched Aaron and liked what he saw. Hank batted and fielded well that day. But Griggs did not like the cross-handed way in which Hank held the bat. During the game Griggs asked Hank if he could hit while holding the bat correctly. Hank said he didn't know. He agreed to give it a try. In his first at-bat while placing his right hand above his left hand, he hit a home run.

Around this time the New York Giants (the team that now plays in San Francisco) also got wind of Hank's batting skill. Contracts from the Braves and the Giants arrived at about the same time. Fans have often wondered how baseball history would have changed had Hank signed with the New York team. He may have become more famous more quickly because New York is a media center. And he also would have played on the same team as Willie Mays, another one of the greatest players of all time.

But Hank chose the Braves for two reasons: They offered more money to start, $350 per month for the Braves versus $250 per month for the Giants, and the Giants misspelled Hank's name "Arron" on the contract. The Braves spelled everything correctly.

Although he was leading the Negro American League in hitting when he signed with the Braves, he went into a slump during the last two weeks he was with the Clowns and was no longer in first place when he left. Taking his leave of the Clowns, Hank boarded an airplane to Eau Claire, Wisconsin, where the Braves' rookie league team played. For the first time, Hank was about to play with white teammates, white opponents, and in front of white fans.

3

HANK THE BRAVE

On June 12, 1952, Hank Aaron arrived at the Eau Claire airport to report to that city's Class C team, the Bears. The minor leagues are divided up by levels, which are named with letters. The level just below the major leagues is called AAA. Below that is AA, followed by A, B, and C. Today everything below A ball is called rookie league.

Some minor leagues start their seasons in June rather than in April because so many of their players are students. This gives the boys a chance to finish the school year without missing any games.

One sportswriter was at the Eau Claire airport to meet Hank, who then checked into the local YMCA. (Forty-two years later, 5,000 people would show up for Aaron's appearance in Eau Claire for the dedication of a statue of Hank at the ballpark where he once played. Aaron recalled that day: "I had goose bumps. A lot of things

Milwaukee Braves' outfielder Hank Aaron (Associated Press)

happened to me in my 23 years as a ballplayer, but nothing touched me more than that day in Eau Claire.") He found that he had two black teammates at Eau Claire, but he was still terribly lonesome. The town was not hateful toward blacks, but, as Hank later put it, "We didn't exactly blend in."

A Rocky Start

Hank's first at-bat in integrated baseball was against Art Rosser, a left-handed pitcher for St. Cloud. He hit a hard single over third base. "I knew everything would be fine," he said. Up until that time in his life, everyone had called him Henry. But as people began to take notice of Hank's talent, the newspapers in Eau Claire began calling him Hank—and he has been Hank ever since.

He played shortstop, but he was not very good at the position. During one of his first games he was trying to turn a double play when his relay throw hit the approaching runner, a white player, right in the forehead, knocking him cold. The player had to be placed on a stretcher and carried off the field. Hank felt horrible. The fans, almost all of whom were white, booed Hank and shouted insults.

A few days later Hank was toying with the idea of becoming a switch hitter, a player who can bat both left- and right-handed. But while practicing his left-handed swing, he accidentally let go of the bat and it flew into the face of a teammate, breaking his nose. Hank shelved the idea of being a switch hitter forever.

Hank was so sad and lonely in Eau Claire that he considered quitting baseball and returning home. He called home and his brother Herbert Jr. answered the phone. Herbert reminded Hank that this was his dream and that he had to stick to it. Hank recalled Jackie Robinson's speech back in Mobile, and how it was important to stick with your dream. He stuck it out.

A Great Hitter

Although Hank did not get much better at playing shortstop, his hitting was tremendous. His batting average for the season was .336. He was named the league's Rookie of the Year. The award was based on a vote taken of local sportswriters. Hank earned more votes than the second-, third-, and fourth-place finishers combined.

Hank's reputation for great hitting would continue throughout his career. One of the reasons Hank was one of the greatest hitters ever was because he rarely thought of anything else during the baseball season. He began thinking about that day's game from the moment he woke up in the morning. Hank believed in studying the pitchers. He studied the way they pitched, the rhythm of their wind-up motion. He noted where their hand was when they released the ball.

He was what is called a "guess hitter." He would guess which pitch the pitcher was going to throw—a fastball, curve, or slider. If he got the pitch he was looking for, he would hit it hard. Sometimes he did not have to guess. Some pitchers would give clues as to what type of pitch they were about to throw. Hank would be able to see the way the pitcher gripped the ball, or the way he started his windup, and know if a fastball or a curve was coming.

Many ballplayers were always tinkering with their swing. They would think about how they shifted their weight from their back foot to the front, where their shoulder was, how they snapped their wrists. But Hank rarely thought about his own swing. His swing remained very much as it had been when he was a boy and he was swinging at bottle caps with a broomstick, except he now held the bat with the correct hand on top. Instead, he thought about the pitcher.

Aaron did not have a long, looping swing like many of today's high-homer, low-average hitters. He generated power with a compact swing because of the strength and quickness of his wrists. If you were a pitcher in the 1950s and '60s, sooner or later you learned the truth about Hank Aaron: He could beat you with his wrists alone.

According to Hank, the two most important words in hitting are confidence and patience. He was confident that he could hit any pitcher in the world, and he was patient enough to wait for a good pitch to hit.

Back to the Clowns

When Hank's first season with the Bears was over, he did not return to Mobile right away. Instead, he rejoined the Indianapolis Clowns. The Negro American League schedule went well into the fall. As the season progressed, the teams just played more games in the South where the weather was better.

The Clowns played in that year's Negro American League World Series, which was a best-of-13 series that traveled from ballpark to ballpark. Best of 13 means that the first team to win seven games won the Negro American League championship. The Clowns' opponents were the Birmingham Black Barons.

One of the Negro American League World Series games was played in Mobile, at Hartwell Field. The game day was declared Henry Aaron Day, and Hank was honored by a local black organization called the Dragon Social Club. For this game, Hank's father did not have to climb a tree in order to watch the match over the fence.

The final game of the World Series was played in New Orleans. The Clowns won their third straight NAL championship. During the series Hank batted .400 and hit five home runs.

Breaking the Color Line

In the spring of 1953 Hank was promoted to the Braves' Class A league team in Jacksonville, Florida—then a hotbed for racism. The Jacksonville Tars played in the South Atlantic League, commonly known as the Sally League. The league had been around since 1904, and until that year there had never been a black ballplayer on any of the league's teams. Hank—along with his teammates Horace Garner and Felix Mantilla and two players on the Savannah, Georgia, team—were to be the first black players to ever play in the Sally League.

The Braves were placing the black players on the Jacksonville roster even though local laws concerning race, called Jim Crow laws, said it was illegal for athletic teams playing in Jacksonville to be integrated.

Like Jackie Robinson before him, Hank was breaking the color line, and he knew he was going to need all of his courage to do it. He knew that he would face physical and verbal assaults and that he would need to be brave enough to not fight back. Hank had to, as he later put it, "pretend he couldn't hear them." Only by keeping his dignity, no matter what, would integration be allowed to continue. White pitchers often threw the ball at Hank's head while he was batting. But Hank just ducked out of the way, dusted himself off, and hit the next pitch over the wall for a home run. White fans continued to scream insults, but black fans (who had to sit in the "Negro Only" sections of the stands) cheered for him.

Hank's first game for Jacksonville was an exhibition game against the Boston Red Sox. Because there would be both black and white ballplayers on the field, the Jacksonville newspaper, the *Florida Times-Union*, called the game a "historic event."

The Red Sox had no trouble defeating the Tars. The final score was 14-1, with Jacksonville's lone run coming from a Hank Aaron home run. Throughout the game, Hank and the other black players had to put up with name-calling from white fans in the stands.

The first regular-season game for the Tars was against Savannah, the other Sally League team that had black ballplayers. The game was in Savannah, and a huge crowd of 5,500 people showed up. It was Savannah's largest baseball crowd in years, and the reason for this was clear to see: For the first time, black fans were coming to see the games, and they were coming in droves.

That season, the Tars quickly proved that they were one of the best teams in the league. They won their first seven games before they lost one. Attendance remained high throughout the season, with many of the clubs setting attendance records. The black sections in the stands, which were very small at the start of the season, had to be enlarged. At first some white fans stopped coming to the ballpark because there were so many black fans. But Hank quickly proved himself to be the best ballplayer Jacksonville had ever seen, and many of the white fans returned to watch him play. Unfortunately there were many white fans who saw the enlarged black section of the stands as an excuse to yell louder and more insulting things at the black ballplayers.

One of the things that made life as a Jacksonville Tar tolerable for Hank was manager Ben Geraghty, a white man who seemed to understand what his black ballplayers were going through. He always saw to it that they had a place to sleep when the team was on the road, so they would not have to sleep on the bus. This usually meant making arrangements with black fans for the players to stay in their homes. When restaurants only served the white ballplayers, Geraghty always made sure that someone sneaked plates of food out to the bus so that all of his players would eat.

That same year the Braves' big-league team moved from Boston to Milwaukee. For many years, Boston had been a two-team town. Both the Red Sox of the American League and the Braves of the National League played there. But in the 1950s, with the introduction of television into American living rooms, baseball teams struggled to find fans, and Boston could no longer support two teams. Milwaukee was the smallest city to have a major league team.

During his season with the Tars, Hank met Barbara Lucas on the way to a local post office. She was a student from Jacksonville who had returned home from Florida A&M University and had signed up to take classes at a local business college. They began to date.

Hank had performed badly as a shortstop during his year at Eau Claire, so with the Tars it was decided that he should try a new position. He was moved to second base. The position is considered easier to play than shortstop. Not as many ground balls are hit in that direction. And, since the shortstop plays between third and second base, while the second baseman plays between second and first, the second baseman's throw to first base is shorter.

Hank, however, proved to be no better at playing second base than he had been at playing shortstop. He made 36 errors during his year in the Sally League. One day late in the season, while playing second base, Hank had to run into short right field to make a catch over his shoulder. A runner at third tried to score but Hank whirled and threw him out at home plate. Billy Southworth, who worked for the Braves, was at the game and reported the play to the major league club. Hank could catch fly balls and he had an arm like a rifle. That planted the seed for moving Hank into the outfield.

When Jacksonville clinched the Sally League pennant—that is, the league championship—the team had a party in a local restaurant. Sadly, the restaurant would not serve Hank and his black teammates. The Tars' general manager gave the black players $50 and told them to have their own party.

That year Hank Aaron was named the Sally League's MVP. He had had one of the greatest years in the league's history. His batting average was .362. He smacked 208 hits, 36 doubles, and 14 triples. He had 125 RBIs (no one else in the league had more than 100) and 22 home runs (the second-best record in the league that year). He was far and away the best overall player in the league, despite his 36 errors.

At the banquet where Hank accepted his MVP award, he asked Barbara to marry him. She said he would have to ask her father. Hank said, "Put him on the phone."

They got married a few days later and then left for Puerto Rico, where the Braves had arranged for Hank to play in a winter baseball league. Although Hank continued to be great with a bat in Puerto Rico, his problems with his glove continued. He continued to play second base, but things did not improve. While in Puerto Rico, Hank was first moved to the outfield.

Just as Braves scout Billy Southworth had predicted, Hank was much better at catching fly balls than he was at catching grounders. Hank did not hit that well when he first arrived in Puerto Rico, however. He was batting only

.125 after two weeks. There was talk of sending Hank back to Mobile. Hank later said that it was a good thing they didn't. If he had returned to Alabama that winter, he certainly would have been drafted into the army and would not have returned to the Braves for at least two years. As it turned out, the draft board passed him by. Hank's hitting improved. He finished the winter-league season third in hitting with an average of .322. He tied for the league lead in home runs with nine. And he was so good as an outfielder that he was told to report to the Braves' big-league spring training camp in 1954.

First Days in the Majors

The year 1954 was a landmark for both Hank and the country. Not only was it Hank's first year in the major leagues, it was also the year his first child, daughter Gaile, was born. On the national scene, 1954 was the year the United States Supreme Court ruled that Jim Crow laws were illegal because they went against the U.S. Constitution.

The Braves' big-league training camp was in St. Petersburg, Florida. They played their home spring-training games at Al Lang Field. Hank was not filled with confidence. He was just 19 years old and not sure he was ready to play in the major leagues. He told Barbara to keep their suitcases packed. He figured that after a few days, the call would come for him to leave St. Petersburg and report to the Braves' minor-league training camp.

But that call never came.

Hank mostly sat on the bench during the first few spring-training games in 1954. Then veteran outfielder Bobby Thomson broke his ankle while sliding into a base. According to Hank, Thomson's leg folded under him as he slid. "It was a horrible thing to watch," Hank later said. Thomson, best known for hitting a home run in 1951 that won the pennant for the New York Giants, would miss the remainder of the season with his injury. Hank took his place in left field.

There were a few days between the last game at Al Lang Field and the opener of the regular season against the Cincinnati Reds in Cincinnati. It was a tradition for the Braves and the Brooklyn Dodgers—Jackie Robinson's team—to barnstorm their way north, playing a game every day in cities like Memphis, Birmingham, Alabama, and Louisville, Kentucky. In 1954 the Braves and the Dodgers played a game in Mobile, so Hank was able to play in front of his family and his hometown friends on the same field as Robinson.

During the short barnstorming tour, the black players from both teams stayed at the same hotels, so Hank always ended up in Jackie's room, sitting quietly in the corner while veteran players such as Robinson, Roy

Campanella, and Don Newcombe would share their wisdom. Most of the time the talk would be about baseball, but social issues, such as how to deal with racism, were also discussed. "That was my college," Hank said.

When Hank first became a Brave he was given uniform number 5. It was not until his second season, in 1955, that Hank requested a uniform with a two-digit number. He was given the number that he was to make famous: 44.

Hank did not get a hit in the first game of the season against the Reds at Cincinnati's Crosley Field. In fact, Hank did not get a hit in his first three games as a Brave. He did not bat his way onto a base until the fourth game of the year, the home opener in Milwaukee against the St. Louis Cardinals. The hit came off of pitcher Vic Raschi, who was approaching the end of his career. A little more than a week later, the Braves were once again facing the Cardinals with Raschi on the mound. During this game, Hank hit the first home run of his major league career. No one in the ballpark that day suspected that a record 754 more home runs would follow.

Hank had played in Wisconsin before, of course, and he found the fans in Milwaukee to be even warmer and friendlier than they had been in Eau Claire. At the time there was a love affair between the Braves and Milwaukee. Attendance was great. The stands were packed for just about every game. But not all of the fans came from Milwaukee. The city was surrounded by smaller towns (such as Green Bay, known for its football team, the Packers) and many fans from those towns came to see the Braves as well.

Hank lived in Milwaukee and took a streetcar to the ballpark, riding right alongside fans. During Hank's first year with the Braves, 2.1 million people came to Milwaukee County Stadium. That set the all-time attendance record for the National League.

Hank hung around mostly with his black teammates, who called him "Little Brother," because he was still a teenager.

Hank's rookie season came to an ugly end in early September 1954. In the second game of a doubleheader in Cincinnati, Hank hit a ball against the wall and was going for a triple. When he slid into third base, his ankle rolled under him just as Bobby Thomson's had in spring training. Hank broke the ankle and had to be carried off the field on a stretcher. He was through for the year. He missed the final 25 games of the season.

Hank only hit 12 home runs during his first year as a Brave. His batting average was .280, which was not bad, but not the numbers of a superstar either. He did not win the Rookie of the Year award—although he did receive one vote.

Milwaukee finished third in an eight-team league. Hank continued to play well in the outfield, but there was little to show that this was the beginning of one of the greatest baseball careers ever.

There were, however, indications that the Braves were about to become a very good team. They had as their star pitcher one of the greatest left-handed pitchers ever, Warren Spahn. And their third baseman was Eddie Mathews, who would also end up being inducted into the Baseball Hall of Fame in Cooperstown.

Because Hank's leg was in a cast, he did not do much during the off-season. He stayed in Mobile and played with his baby daughter. He used his baseball earnings to buy a new car, a Pontiac convertible. By the time spring rolled around, the cast was off and Hank was ready to report to St. Petersburg.

Sophomore Year

Hank's hitting statistics improved greatly during his second year with the Braves. He switched to playing right field, where he was to remain for most of his career.

During a game at the Polo Grounds in New York against the Giants, Hank hit a mammoth home run that flew into the upper deck in left field. A New York sportswriter described him in the next day's newspaper as "Hammerin' Hank"—and the name stuck.

Hank was named to the 1955 National League All-Star team, an honor he would receive every year that he played from then on. When his statistics were added up at the end of the year, he had 106 RBIs, a .314 batting average, and 27 home runs. The Braves, still improving, finished second in the National League—behind the great Brooklyn Dodgers team.

In 1955 Hank hit more than 20 home runs for the first time. He would do it again for the next 19 seasons.

Today, baseball players are paid millions of dollars. But that was hardly the case in 1955. Most players were paid so little that they had to take jobs during the summer—sometimes playing baseball, sometimes doing other things. Between the 1955 and 1956 baseball seasons Hank made some extra money barnstorming with a team of black major-league all-stars led by Willie Mays. The team traveled from town to town with a team of Negro League all-stars. Mays's team *never* lost. The players rode to each town in cars, and Hank got to ride in Mays's Cadillac. Hank made more money playing for the all-star team, about $3,500 a month, than he did playing for the Braves.

After that Hank returned to Mobile with his family and took a job working with the local recreation department, the same department that had run the softball league he had played in when he was a child.

A Solid Season

In 1956 Hank received a raise. He earned $17,000 a year, so he would not have to work during the summer anymore. The Braves were now considered one of the best teams in the league and a strong candidate to win the pennant.

At one point, the Braves won 11 straight games and pushed their way into first place. Everyone in Wisconsin went Braves crazy. Restaurants named sandwiches after the team. Stores in Milwaukee put "We Love the Braves" signs in their windows. "I believe we should have won the pennant that year but we choked," Hank later said.

They had a chance to clinch the pennant with a victory over the Cardinals in St. Louis. It was a Saturday afternoon game at the end of the season. The Braves put their best pitcher, Warren Spahn, on the mound. After 12 innings the score was tied 1-1, and Spahn was still pitching. The Cardinals' starting pitcher, Herm Wehmeier, was also still in the game. The Cardinals won the game in the 13th inning when a ground ball took a bad hop and got past third baseman, Eddie Mathews.

"Beyond a doubt, that Saturday game in St. Louis was the most heartbreaking moment I had in 21 years of baseball," Spahn later said.

The Braves once again finished in second place in the National League, behind the Brooklyn Dodgers. Hank batted .328, the best average in the league. At age 22 he was baseball's second-youngest batting champion ever.

People were starting to recognize Aaron as one of baseball's great hitters, but not as one of baseball's great home run hitters. According to teammate Warren Spahn, people thought Hank might one day hit .400, something no one had been able to do since the Boston Red Sox's Ted Williams did in 1941. Hank hit hard line drives, not towering fly balls like most home run hitters.

In 1956 Hank came in third place in the voting for National League MVP, but he was named the National League Player of the Year by the bible of baseball, a magazine called *The Sporting News*.

Quietly Building a Reputation

It took baseball fans outside of Milwaukee a long time to figure out just how good Hank was. Years later when Hank began to approach Babe Ruth's home run record, many fans were caught by surprise.

That was partly because Hank was a quiet man, who seldom drew attention to himself off the baseball field. Another reason was that he entered the major leagues a couple of years behind Willie Mays, another home run hitting black outfielder.

Mays played the first years of his career in New York, where the press made him famous in a way the Milwaukee press could not do for Hank. Mays, like Aaron, was one of the greatest players ever, but Mays was a flashier player who tended to do things with flair. For example, his hat tended to fly off his head while he was running to catch fly balls. Hank, on the other hand, made hard plays look easy, so fans were not as impressed by him.

The Braves started the 1957 season like a team on a mission. On opening day, they beat the Cincinnati Reds 1-0. Braves pitcher Lew Burdette pitched the entire game, and the only run of the game was a Hank Aaron home run. Two days later Hank had five hits in five times at bat. He had four runs batted in the game after that. The next day, in a 2-1 victory over the Dodgers, Hank drove in both Braves' runs with his red-hot bat. The Braves won nine of their first 10 games.

The Braves were on fire and so was Hank. During one stretch in June Hank hit seven home runs in eight days.

It was about this time that Hank first realized that the players who hit for a high batting average did not get the same fame, or the same paycheck, as the guys who hit a lot of home runs. He says he did not change his swing or his hitting style at that point in his career, but he did begin to hit more home runs. Hank thinks it was because he was a little bit older, stronger, and smarter. One thing was for sure: Instead of hitting the ball to all fields, a method that would give him the highest possible batting average, Hank began to wait for pitches that were on the inside part of the plate, pitches he could pull to left field. That was the way power hitters—home-run hitters—went about the task.

Hank's goal during the 1957 season was to win the Triple Crown, which means to lead the league in batting average, home runs, and runs batted in. Mickey Mantle of the New York Yankees had done it in 1956 in the American League, and he had become a national hero in the process.

New York Yankee Mickey Mantle and Milwaukee Brave Hank Aaron in 1958 (Associated Press)

Then came a very bad day in early July. Two of the Braves outfielders, Bill Bruton and Felix Mantilla, collided while trying to catch the same fly ball. The double injury was painful for Hank because the injured men had been his two best friends on the team. Mantilla, Hank's old teammate from the Jacksonville days, was the godfather of Gaile, Hank's first daughter.

When the collision occurred, Hank was out of the lineup with a sprained ankle. He was supposed to stay off the ankle for two weeks, but the team was suddenly short on outfielders. Hank was pressed back into action before he was ready. He was moved to center field, the toughest of the outfield positions to play, and he stayed there for the rest of the year.

Playing on his injured ankle hurt Hank's ability to hit. He went into a slump until the ankle healed and lost his chance to win the Triple Crown.

In August the Braves had another hot streak. At one point during the month they won 10 games in a row.

Winning the Pennant

On the second-to-last day of the season the Braves needed one more victory over the St. Louis Cardinals to win the pennant. The game was played on a cold night in Milwaukee.

The Braves came close to scoring inning after inning but had trouble getting base runners home. Several times they made the third out with the bases loaded. The game was tied after nine innings and went into extra innings.

In the 11th inning the Braves got one man on base, with Hank coming up to bat. On the mound for the Cardinals was right-handed relief pitcher Billy Muffett. Muffett was known for his curve ball and was considered very tough to hit. In fact, he had not given up a home run all year.

Hank came to the plate envisioning Muffett's curve ball: how he threw it, how the ball bent in midair, the speed at which he threw it. When Muffett threw the very curve ball that Hank had been envisioning, he was ready for it. Hank hit the ball to straightaway center field, and the ball went over the wall into a grove of trees.

Hank's home run won the game, and the pennant, for the Braves. Hank later said that his baseball career did not get any better than that. He said he felt as if he had been named "king of Wisconsin." All his teammates were waiting for him at home plate. They lifted him up onto their shoulders and carried him off the field.

Hank ended the regular season realizing two-thirds of his Triple Crown dream. He hit 44 home runs, beating out Ernie Banks of the Chicago Cubs, who hit 43. He also led the league in runs batted in, with 132. But he finished a distant second to St. Louis Cardinals legend Stan Musial in batting average, hitting .322 to Musial's .351.

The 1957 World Series

In the 1957 World Series the Braves played the super team of the 1950s, the New York Yankees. Considered one of the greatest teams of all times, the Yankees had four future Hall of Famers on their squad: outfielders Mickey Mantle and Enos Slaughter, catcher Yogi Berra, and pitcher Whitey Ford.

Although the Braves matched up in terms of talent, the Yankees represented the largest city in the major leagues, while the Braves represented the smallest. This gave the World Series a "David versus Goliath" feel. The Braves' feelings toward the Yankees turned to a solid dislike after some of the Yankee players referred to Milwaukee as a "bush league town"—in other words, a small-time town— in the newspapers.

The series started in New York. The teams split the first two games in Yankee Stadium. Then the teams moved to Milwaukee for the first World Series game ever played in that city. The matchup did not go well for the hometown fans. Both of the game's highlights for the Braves involved Aaron.

Hank, still playing center field because of Bruton's injury, made a sliding catch of a line drive. Later he hit a two-run home run. But other than that things went the Yankees' way, and they took a two-games-to-one lead in the series.

The following day Hank hit a three-run home run. This shot is considered one of the hardest balls he ever hit, because it made it out of the ballpark even though there was a stiff wind blowing in. But it was the Braves' third baseman, Eddie Mathews, who was the hero of the game, hitting a home run to win the game for Milwaukee. This tied the series at two games apiece.

The fifth game, also in Milwaukee, was a pitcher's duel, with Lew Burdette of the Braves outpitching Whitey Ford of the Yankees and winning the game 1-0.

Needing only one more victory to become world champions, the series moved back to New York. Hank hit another home run in Game 6, but the Braves lost. That meant that Game 7 would be the showdown between both teams.

The game was played on October 10, 1957. The Braves were scheduled to pitch their ace Warren Spahn for the final game, but Spahn had the flu. So Burdette took his place and pitched on only two days' rest. Pitching for the Yankees was Don Larsen, who had become famous the previous fall by pitching the only perfect game (27 batters, 27 outs) in World Series history. But on this day Burdette was far closer to perfect than Larsen. The Braves won the game 5-0 and became the world champions. Milwaukee erupted in joy.

During the series Hank had hit three home runs, knocked in seven runs, and batted .393. A few weeks later Hank was named MVP for the 1957 National League season.

The year 1957 was great for Hank in a couple of ways. Not only did he lead his team to the world championship, but his wife Barbara also gave birth to his first son, Henry Jr., just before the season started.

Hank, Hank Jr., and Barbara at home in 1957 (Corbis)

Following the Braves' victory, Mobile arranged to have another Hank Aaron Day. The Aarons took the train to Mobile and were met at the station by a marching band that played "Take Me out to the Ball Game." A limousine was waiting to take them in a motorcade to the Colored Elks Club, where the mayor of Mobile, Joseph Langan, gave Hank the key to the city.

It does not seem that racism still should have been much of a problem for the reigning World Series MVP and National League batting champ. But nothing could have been further from the truth. Despite his accomplishments, Hank still could not eat in the same restaurant with his teammates during spring training in Florida, nor could he stay in the same hotel. When Hank was invited to speak at white clubs in Mobile, he asked if he could bring his father along. The clubs said no, so Hank canceled his appearances.

That same spring a group of white teenagers ran Hank and teammate Felix Mantilla off a road at 60 miles per hour. Hank and Felix were frightened but unhurt by the incident.

4

SWINGING FOR THE FENCES

In 1958 the Braves won their second National League pennant in a row. They finished the season eight games in front of the second-place team, the Pittsburgh Pirates. The Braves won 92 games to the Pirates 84. The Braves clinched the pennant in a game during mid-September against the Cincinnati Reds. The winning hit was a two-run home run by Hank Aaron.

It looked like the Braves were going to easily defend their world championship. After four games the Braves led the series three games to one. One more victory and they would be two-time world champs. But it was not to be.

The Yankees refused to be beaten after that and won three straight games, including two in Milwaukee. It was one of history's closest World Series, with each of the seven games being decided by one run.

Hank had 11 hits in the 1957 Series. He added nine more World Series hits in 1958. At the time he thought this would be the start of a beautiful streak of World Series appearances, but this was pure fantasy. Despite the fact that he would play in the major leagues for another 18 years, Hank Aaron would never play in another World Series game.

At the end of the year, Hank won his first Gold Glove Award, honoring him as one of the best outfielders in baseball. His coaches and managers would have thought such a thing was impossible back in the days when he was still trying to be an infielder.

With 30 home runs and a .326 batting average, he also finished third in the MVP voting for the National League that year, behind only Ernie Banks of the Chicago Cubs and Willie Mays of the San Francisco Giants, both of whom are also African Americans.

In 1958, exactly nine months after Hank Jr. was born, Barbara gave birth to twin boys, Gary and Lary. Sadly, the twins were born prematurely and Gary died soon after birth.

Buckling Down for a Great Season

In 1959 Hank stopped going to the movies with his teammates. He felt that it was bad for his eyes and would make him less of a great hitter. It must have worked too, because according to Hank, he was never a better hitter than he was during the 1959 season.

During the first six weeks of the season Hank was batting .450, getting a hit just about every other time he came to the plate. Newspapers again began to talk about the possibility of Aaron hitting .400 for the season.

The year 1959 was also a landmark year in the integration of baseball. It was the first year that every major league team had at least one African American on its roster. The Boston Red Sox were the final team to integrate.

On a cold Milwaukee night in May the Braves played in one of the most famous games in baseball history. Their opponents were the Pittsburgh Pirates. The Braves had Lew Burdette on the mound. The Pirates' pitcher that night was Harvey Haddix—and it would come to be known as "the Harvey Haddix game."

After 12 innings the game was knotted in a scoreless tie, and both Burdette and Haddix were still in the game. But Haddix's performance was truly exceptional. He was pitching a perfect game. In other words, he had faced 36 Braves and had gotten all of them out. No other pitcher had ever done this.

Sadly for Haddix, the Braves scored in the 13th inning and ended up winning the game. Gone was Haddix's perfect game, gone was the no-hitter, gone was the shutout, and gone was the Pirates' win. The Braves felt great. They had not sent a single base runner in 12 innings and they still won the game.

One of the highlights of Hank's career came in June 1959 when he hit three home runs in a game for the only time in his career. He did it against San Francisco Giants pitcher Johnny Antonelli. Antonelli threw a pitch near Hank's head early in the game, which made Hank angry. By the time the game was over, Antonelli was no doubt regretting that high and inside pitch.

In those days the players voted for the all-stars to play in the annual All-Star game. Today the fans do the voting. But in 1959 Aaron became the only player ever to be voted unanimously onto the All-Star team.

Losing the Pennant

When the 1959 season ended, the Braves and the Los Angeles Dodgers were tied for first place. A three-game playoff was played to determine the pennant winner. Whereas five years earlier the Braves were selling out most of their games, by 1959 Milwaukee had stopped caring about the team. Despite the importance of the post-season playoff, more than half the stands were empty for the Braves' home game. Although the weather was bad that day that had not stopped the fans from coming before. Hank believed that Milwaukee had begun to take the Braves for granted.

The Dodgers won that first game in Milwaukee and the teams moved to Los Angeles for Game 2. The Braves lost the playoff to the Dodgers, and Los Angeles went on to the World Series.

Playing right field, Hank made the game's best defensive play, a running catch of a Junior Gilliam line drive just before he slammed into the wall. With two outs and two men on base, the catch saved a couple of runs. The game was scoreless after 11 innings, but the Dodgers scored in the bottom of the 12th to win the series and the National League pennant.

Hank later said, "The Braves were good enough to win at least four pennants in a row. In the record book, we're just a team that won a World Series. We were better than that."

The loss to the Dodgers in the three-game playoff took something from the Braves—something they never got back. The team would not get that close to winning the National League pennant for another 10 years.

Home Run Derby

In 1959 Hank knew he was a good hitter—one of the best hitters around, in fact. He finished the 1959 season with a batting average of .355, winning his second batting title. He was 25 years old and had more than 1,000 career hits.

He was the second-youngest player to reach the 1,000-hit mark. Only Ty Cobb was younger. But Hank still did not think of himself as a home run hitter, and certainly not as a player who would one day be crowned the Home Run King of baseball.

All that changed that year when Hank was invited to be on a syndicated TV show called *Home Run Derby*. The show was filmed in Los Angeles' Wrigley Field (not to be confused with Chicago's Wrigley Field). This park was the original home of the Los Angeles (now Anaheim) Angels. Hosted by Mark Scott, the half-hour show pitted two sluggers against one another to see who could hit the most home runs off of batting practice (slower) pitches. (The game is now played every year the day before the All-Star game, but in 1959 it was new.)

Home Run Derby was an elimination tournament held in rounds. Hank not only did very well, he also won the entire competition. He received $30,000 for his victory, which was more than he was paid for a whole season of playing with the Braves. With his victory, Hank stopped thinking of himself as just a good hitter, and began to think of himself as a good power hitter.

He also understood more than ever that hitting home runs was the path to financial security. "They never had a show called *Singles Derby*," he joked.

"Supe"

Perhaps Hank's realization further changed his approach at the plate, but for whatever reason, his home run numbers started to grow in the seasons that followed *Home Run Derby*. He hit 40 home runs and knocked in 126 runs in 1960. The Braves were still a much-better-than-average team that season, but they finished second to the Pittsburgh Pirates.

Hank hit 34 home runs with 120 RBIs in 1961—but the Braves fell to fourth place. Their lineup could still hit with the best teams, but their pitching staff was nothing compared to what it had been when they were one of the best teams in the world.

Hank hit 40 home runs with 126 RBIs in 1962. That season Hank hit the longest home run of his career. The Braves were playing the brand-new team in New York, the Mets, at the Polo Grounds, the same ballpark that the Giants had used. Hank hit the long-distance shot off Mets pitcher Jay Hook; the ball came down 470 feet from home, in the bleachers.

The Braves fell another spot in the standings in 1962, finishing in fifth place. Now there were more National League teams finishing ahead of the Braves than there were finishing behind them.

That year Hank made $50,000, which he considered more than enough. The Aaron family had a new color

TV, when most people still had black-and-white sets. They lived in a nice house in Milwaukee with a patio that was shaped like a ballpark. Above the fireplace in the den was an autographed photo of President John F. Kennedy that the president had sent to Hank after Hank campaigned for him in 1960. That year Hank's daughter Dorinda was born on Hank's birthday.

It was also the first year that Hank's brother Tommie played for the Braves. Tommie Aaron, who was five years younger than Hank, played part-time at first base with the Braves until 1971. He lived in Hank's house when the Braves were home, and the brothers were roommates when the team was on the road. Although Tommie only hit 13 home runs in his big-league career, together he and Hank hit the most home runs by any pair of brothers: 768.

In 1963 the Braves moved their spring training camp to West Palm Beach, Florida. Although there was still a "colored section" at the ballpark, all of the players could now stay at the same hotel.

Hank hit 44 home runs (the same number as his uniform) with 130 RBIs in 1963. With his legs feeling better than they had in years, Hank set out to show that he was a complete ballplayer. He began to steal bases, and he quickly proved that he was good at it. He stole 31 bases during the year, and was only thrown out while trying to steal five times. He finished second in the league in steals.

Hank (left) and his brother Tommie Aaron hold the record for hitting the most home runs by any pair of brothers: 768. (Corbis)

Also that season, Hank came closer than he ever had (or ever would) to winning the Triple Crown. He tied for the league lead in homers with San Francisco Giant Willie McCovey, led the league in RBIs, and his batting average, .319, was second only to Tommy Davis of the Dodgers.

Each year, his offensive output was a little more impressive than it had been the year before. But again the Braves dropped in the standings, finishing sixth.

In 1964 the Braves did a little better. They finished in fifth place, but only five games behind the pennant-winning Cardinals. Hank hit for a .328 batting average, but his home runs dropped off to 24 that year.

Around this time Hank realized he was not having as much fun playing baseball as he once had. One by one, all of his teammates from his early years with the Braves left the team. He went from being "Little Brother," a teenager on a team full of grown men, to the veteran who was by far the team's most famous player. His nickname now was "Supe," which was short for Superstar.

Good-bye, Milwaukee

Unfortunately, Milwaukee's interest in baseball continued to decline. As Hank's numbers rose, attendance figures at Milwaukee County Stadium dropped. During the early 1960s the Braves failed to draw as many as 1 million fans per year. The team that had once set the National League attendance record now finished last in attendance.

Sensing that the Braves would soon be looking for another place to play, the governor of Georgia, Carl Sanders, arranged to have a major league ballpark built in Atlanta. The 1965 season was the Braves' last in Milwaukee.

Hank missed the first three weeks of the season because of an ankle operation. The Braves played much better and came close to winning the pennant. That did not help attendance, however. Milwaukee fans knew that the Braves were moving out of town the next year. They were not going to support a team that was deserting them. Hank had 32 homers and batted .318 in 1965.

That year Aaron and Eddie Mathews broke the record for most home runs hit by a pair of teammates. Babe Ruth and Lou Gehrig had set the record of 793 homers while playing together on the New York Yankees of the 1920s and 1930s. Before Mathews was traded following the 1966 season, he and Hank hit 863 home runs as teammates.

Hank loved Milwaukee and was heartbroken over the Braves leaving town. He later said, "Whenever I'm in Milwaukee, which is often, I'm reminded that the people there still haven't gotten over the Braves leaving. If it helps, they should know that the players haven't either."

Hello, Atlanta

In 1966 the Milwaukee Braves became the Atlanta Braves—and the team has remained in Atlanta ever since. Hank finished his career as a Milwaukee Brave with 398 home runs. The Braves lost their first game in Atlanta 3-2 to the Pittsburgh Pirates. It was not a memorable game but Hank did steal the first base in Atlanta Braves history.

Hank's new home ballpark, Atlanta Fulton County Stadium, had a small playing field. Baseball, unlike other sports, does not have a rule determining how large a playing field should be. Some parks have the outfield fences far from home plate. At others, the fences are closer to the batters. In Atlanta, not only were the fences close, but the stadium also was built at a high altitude and the weather was often very hot. These factors tend to make baseballs travel farther. The Atlanta Stadium soon earned a reputation as a home run hitter's paradise. For this reason, its nickname became "The Launching Pad."

When reviewing Hank's stellar career, critics are quick to point out the advantages that the Atlanta Fulton County Stadium presented, saying that these gave Hank an unfair advantage. But those critics never mention that Milwaukee County Stadium, where Hank played for the first half of his career, was not a good park for hitting home runs. The fences were farther out and the weather was often cold. During his years as a Milwaukee Brave, Hank always hit more home runs during road games than he did at home. (Major League Baseball teams play a 162-game season, with 81 games at home and 81 on the road.) It was not until he had played in Atlanta for six years that his career totals equaled out, and he hit as many home runs at home as he had on the road.

The Braves and Hank moved from Milwaukee to Atlanta in 1966. (National Baseball Hall of Fame Library, Cooperstown, NY)

Soon after he began playing in Atlanta Hank whacked his 400th home run. But the move to Atlanta was not entirely joyous for Hank. When he returned to the South, Hank was again heckled by racists. Hank was also having problems at home. He and wife Barbara separated. A fire destroyed his home, and with it many of the trophies he had won over the years. His dog also died in the fire. Hank went to the baseball field to get away from his troubles—at least most of the time. Hank also had feuds with teammates and with the team's radio announcer.

In 1966 the Braves won more games than they lost for the 14th straight year, but they did not win enough to come close to winning the pennant. Hank's batting average slipped to .279 that year. Hank said that it was because the Georgia heat wore him down. But he hit a league-leading 44 home runs, again matching his uniform number. He also led the league in RBIs with 127.

Hank was now making $100,000 a year, one of only six players earning that much money. The others were Mickey Mantle, Don Drysdale, Sandy Koufax, Willie Mays, and Frank Robinson.

After the 1966 season Hank toured Vietnam, where the United States was involved in a war. He made appearances for the troops along with a group of other baseball stars. When the group returned to the United States they visited the White House, where they met President Lyndon Johnson, the first of three presidents Hank would meet.

In 1967 the Braves lost more games than they won for the first time since 1953. Also in 1967, Oliver Kuechle, who edited the sports page for the *Milwaukee Journal,* was the first reporter to mention that Hank might have a shot at breaking Babe Ruth's career 714 home runs record.

Hank again led the league in homers that year, smacking 39 of them. And his batting average improved over the previous season, rising to .307.

500th Home Run

The 1968 baseball season started amid racial upheaval in America. Civil rights activist Dr. Martin Luther King Jr., recently assassinated in Memphis, was buried in Atlanta the day before the Braves played their home opener. Dr. King's father came to the ballgame. Elsewhere, there were race riots throughout the United States.

Hank hit his 500th home run on July 14, 1968, in Atlanta. He was 35 years old. It turned out to be an understatement after the game when Hank told reporters, "I think I still have a few [home runs] left in me."

He hit the homer off pitcher Mike McCormick of the San Francisco Giants. There were two men on base when Hank hit his home run, and those three RBIs helped the Braves to a 4-2 win. His teammates ran out of the dugout and mobbed Hank as he crossed home plate.

"I don't have any special goals but if I can stay healthy and everything, I think I can hit well over 600 before I quit," he told reporters. "I haven't been thinking about hitting home runs. I've just been in a slump, that's all."

He received a standing ovation from the Atlanta crowd of 34,283. His teammates also celebrated with him on the field.

"That was great, the way the guys greeted me," Hank said. "It means a lot to have them and the fans behind you like that. I wanted to hit my 500th here; I didn't want to do it on the road. Also, I wanted it to come in a win. I was guessing fastball," he said, "and that's what he threw. I remember a game last year where he struck me out three times with fast balls, so I figured that's the way he'd be throwing. I'm glad I hit it off a guy like McCormick. After all, he won the Cy Young Award last year. It feels better when you hit one off a great pitcher like that."

The only disappointment for Hank was that his 67-year-old father did not get to see it. Herbert Aaron had been in Atlanta for three days to see the feat, but was on a plane back to Mobile when Hank finally put one over the fence.

After hitting number 500, Hank became the first ballplayer to have his own night in Atlanta. The first of several Hank Aaron nights was held at the ballpark in August 1968.

Hank hits his 500th home run. (National Baseball Hall of Fame Library, Cooperstown, NY)

Getting Older, Getting Better

In addition to possessing skill, Hank became one of the greatest baseball players in history through discipline and fitness. During his 23 years as a major league ballplayer, he was always in shape and rarely injured. When Hank reached his late thirties, a time when most men's baseball skills are quickly diminishing, he continued to sock home runs with the league leaders. He hit 40 home runs at the age of 40.

By 1969 Hank's days of trying to hit .400 were behind him. Because he almost always hit the ball toward left field, opposing teams sometimes positioned their players strangely to make it harder for Hank to get hits. Some teams would play three infielders on the left side of the infield. In other words, the second baseman would move to the "wrong" side of second base, leaving the first baseman all alone to cover the right side of the infield. Other teams would put the second baseman in short left field so that they were using four outfielders against Hank. But there is no way to defend against home runs. Many teams found themselves helplessly watching as Hank's hit sailed over the fence. There was no way for teams to position their players higher off the ground.

In 1969 the Braves were a top-notch ball club once again. Although Hank was having trouble with a bad back, the pain was not enough to keep him off the field.

"It was great fun to win again," Hank said.

New Playoff System

The 1969 season was the first to be played under a new playoff format. Up until that time the team with the best regular season record in the American League won the pennant. That team played the team with the best record in the National League in the World Series to decide baseball's world champion.

In 1969 the two leagues each split into two divisions. The winners of each division played each other in a best-of-five game series to decide who would play against the other league's winner in the World Series. (Today the leagues each have three divisions, and one wild-card team makes it into postseason play. There are two levels of playoffs, the League Divisions Series and the League Championship Series, before a team can get to the World Series.)

In 1969 the Braves clinched their division on the final Saturday of the season with a win over the Cincinnati Reds. That night Hank and the rest of the Braves, as Hank later put it, "partied way too much." Hank locked himself out of his house and cut his hand breaking a window to get in. He was going to have to play his first postseason games since 1958 with stitches in his hand. Because they did not want people to know the real story, the Braves told the press that Hank had cut his hand on a fence while playing with his dog.

The Braves' opponents were the New York Mets. They were called Miracle Mets, because only a few years earlier they had been one of the worst teams in baseball history. The Braves dropped three straight games to the Mets, but none of the losses were Hank's fault. The stitches, as it turned out, had no effect on his hitting. He hit a home run in each of the Braves' three losses, and batted .357 against a great Mets pitching staff led by future Hall of Famer Tom Seaver.

3,000th Hit

There are certain milestones for baseball players that, if reached, ensure that player's induction into the Baseball Hall of Fame. For pitchers, winning 300 games does the trick. For power hitters, whacking 500 homers opens the door to Cooperstown. Hank had already done that.

For hitters without power, making more than 3,000 hits is the key. Hank, of course, had plenty of power—but he always hit plenty of singles and doubles as well. Babe Ruth never made it to the 3,000-hit mark, but Hank whacked his 3,000th hit relatively early in his career, on May 17, 1970. Hank became the ninth player to make 3,000 hits—and the first to ever hit both 500 home runs and 3,000 hits.

The hit came off of Cincinnati right-hander Wayne Simpson. The ground ball never made it out of the infield, but Hank ran hard and beat the throw to first base. The game was stopped as the scoreboard showed Aaron's achievement. The first baseman gave Hank the ball.

Hall of Famer Stan Musial, who had been sitting next to the Braves' dugout, hopped the fence and ran out onto the field to congratulate Hank. Photographers also came on to the field to capture the moment. They asked Hank to kiss the ball, and he did.

"I'm not used to this much attention," Hank told the swarm of reporters around his locker after the game. "I'm glad it's finally over. I haven't had much rest since I got to within five hits of 3,000."

The Braves had been so sure that Hank's 3,000th hit would be a home run that they placed their equipment manager outside the stadium to retrieve the ball. (Hit number 3,001 *was* a home run.)

The Braves held another Hank Aaron Day to celebrate the 3,000-hit milestone. As congratulatory gifts, Hank received a year's supply of Coca-Cola, a golf cart with the number 44 on it, and a dog.

Hank played much of the 1970 season with a sore knee, which he had injured sliding into home. He refused to have an operation on the knee, which would have caused him to sit out most of the year. Instead, he had it drained six times to keep the swelling down.

Hank continued to hit well, however, despite the knee. He finished the year with 38 home runs. He had 118 RBIs and batted .298. His teammate Rico Carty led the league in hitting with a .366 average, but the Braves did not play

Hank and Willie Mays (of the San Francisco Giants) get together for a chat before the All-Star game in Cincinnati, Ohio, in 1970. (Associated Press)

winning baseball. They lost more than they won and finished fifth in their six-team division.

For a time during his off-seasons Hank had become a hunter. Like many ballplayers, he enjoyed deer, duck, and pheasant hunting. But after a few years he lost his enjoyment. "I didn't have much stomach for shooting things," he later said.

In February 1971, Hank's divorce from Barbara became final.

600th Home Run

During the first month of the 1971 season Hank passed another milestone by hitting his 600th home run. The homer came off of future Hall of Famer Gaylord Perry of the San Francisco Giants. Before the game Perry said, "If Hank Aaron hits his 600th home run off me, he is going to have to earn it!" Hank was looking forward to getting his 600th off Perry because the veteran pitcher had long been suspected of throwing a spitball, which is against the rules.

"I regarded a spitball as cheating," Hank later said.

The pitch Hank hit was not a spitball though. It was a fastball in the third inning, and Hank hit it over the left-field fence. Perry kicked the dirt as Aaron rounded the bases. A small Atlanta crowd of 13,494 gave Hank a standing ovation.

The Giants' center fielder, Willie Mays—who also had 600 home runs on his resume—said after the game: "He's not through rocking this place yet. If you think they [the fans] got shook up tonight, tell 'em just to stick around."

"It would have been sweeter," said Hank, "if we had won."

The Giants won the game 6-5 on a scoring single in the 10th inning by Mays.

In 1971 Hank hit 47 home runs—his highest total yet—despite his sore knee, which again caused him to miss quite a few games.

5

CHASING THE BABE

In 1972 Hank met the woman who would become his second wife. She was Billye Williams, an Atlanta TV talk-show host. Billye was a recent widow with a young daughter named Ceci. Her husband had been a minister who was heavily involved in the civil rights movement. Her show was called *Today in Georgia*.

She met Hank while doing a series of interviews with Braves ballplayers called "Billye at the Bat." After many, many telephone conversations (because Hank was on the road so much), he and Billye began to date. Through her, Hank met leaders of the civil rights movement such as Rev. Jesse Jackson.

Continuing Success and Old Challenges

In 1972 Hank signed a new two-year contract with the Braves. He was to be paid $200,000 per year. That season

Hank hit home run number 660, which tied him with Babe Ruth for most home runs hit by one player for the same team. (Although Ruth had 714 home runs in his career, only 660 were as a Yankee. He also hit home runs for the Boston Red Sox and the Boston Braves.)

With Hank's newfound riches came bad investments. Hank lost more than $1 million before he decided that he would never again invest money in something without first consulting his lawyer.

Late in the 1972 season Hank's sagging enjoyment of baseball received a boost when his old longtime teammate Eddie Mathews was named the Braves' new manager. That same year Hank also began what would become a long and successful career in charity fund raising. He held a celebrity bowling tournament, the proceeds from which went to sickle-cell anemia research, a fatal disease that plagues African Americans.

Aaron was not the only player chasing Ruth's career home run record. Also in pursuit was Willie Mays, whose total was also in the 600s. Each time either one of the two players hit a home run it made news.

The chase to break the record was on. But Willie's numbers were starting to shrink. Mays, who played most of his career with the New York and then San Francisco Giants before being traded to the New York Mets for the 1973 season, was beginning to show his age.

It became clear that Mays was not going to break Ruth's record. Hank, on the other hand, was healthy and hitting as well as ever. By the beginning of the 1973 season the spotlight was on Hank alone.

In the fall of 1972 Hank's hero, Jackie Robinson, died. Hank attended Robinson's funeral, but was shocked that only a few active ballplayers were there. "It made me more determined than ever to keep Jackie's dream alive," he later said.

As the 1973 season began Hank was only 41 home runs shy of Ruth's record. That same year Hank received 930,000 cards and letters in the mail. That is a record for anyone other than the president of the United States. Hank was getting so much mail that the Braves hired a secretary to handle it for him.

Sadly, not all of the letters came from supporters. Some letters were filled with racial hatred and were written by people who did not want Hank to break Babe Ruth's record. Hank said that the hate mail made him a better hitter. He channeled all of his anger into his hitting stroke. But the hateful situation soon grew worse. Hank's parents and his children began to receive threatening phone calls.

The FBI was called in. Hank received a police escort to and from the ballpark. A plot to kidnap his daughter Gaile, who was then attending Fisk University, was uncovered. She received FBI protection.

When on the road, Hank began to register in hotels under fake names. One night in Montreal a firecracker went off in the stands and, for a moment, Hank thought someone was shooting at him.

Despite the national attention being given to Hank's home run chase, the fans in Atlanta did not seem to care. During the first half of the 1973 season, an average of only 8,000 fans showed up per game in Atlanta. When Hank played on the road, he was a major attraction and an average of 25,000 fans showed up for those games.

Most fans were there to root for him—but a few showed up to root against him. Once, at the Atlanta ballpark, racist hecklers became so foul that Hank had to call security guards, who escorted the loud-mouthed racists out of the ballpark.

"It should have been the most enjoyable time of my life, and instead it was hell," Hank said.

700th Home Run

On July 21, 1973, Aaron hit his 700th home run. The pitcher was Ken Brett of the Philadelphia Phillies. The ball traveled more than 400 feet into Atlanta's left-field bleachers. The home run took place in the third inning of an 8-4 loss to the Phillies. Even though they lost, the Braves celebrated with champagne in the clubhouse after the game.

The ball was caught by 18-year-old Robert Winborne, a soon-to-be freshman at the University of North Carolina. The Braves gave the young man $700 in exchange for the ball. Winborne offered to give the money to Aaron's favorite charity.

"No, you keep it!" Aaron told him.

It was Aaron's 27th home run of the season, which had more than two full months to go. There were 16,236 people in the stadium to witness the blast. They cheered so long after Hank disappeared into the dugout that he was forced to come back out and tip his cap to the crowd.

Braves teammate Darrell Evans, who was on base when Hank hit number 700, said Aaron was shaking when he crossed home plate.

"It was the first time I've seen him become really emotional," Evans said.

After the game Hank said, "I like to get to those nice, round figures. Now I can start counting down. I only need 14 more, and that doesn't seem like too many. I think maybe I can [break Ruth's record] this season now."

Late in the 1973 season Hank finally told a reporter about the hate mail he had been receiving and the story made newspapers around the country. Although the hate mail did not stop, it was joined by thousands of letters praising Hank.

Number 714

Hank had hoped to break Ruth's record during the 1973 season, but it was not to be. After hitting number 700, he went into a home run slump. There were 10 days between 700 and 701, and another 15 days between 701 and 702. Interest in Atlanta dropped to next to zero. On the night that Hank hit number 711, there were only 1,362 people in Atlanta Fulton County Stadium—the smallest crowd in Braves history.

Hank ended the season just one home run shy of Ruth's 714. The Braves played the last game of the season at home, and the game was sold out. There was not an empty seat in the stadium. Even though Hank popped out in his last at-bat, he received a standing ovation anyway.

During the off-season between the 1973 and '74 seasons, Hank married Billye. They spent their honeymoon in Jamaica. Soon thereafter, Hank adopted Ceci, bringing his number of children to six. He also kept busy going to banquets in his honor, and making guest appearances on many TV shows.

Anticipating Hank's breaking of Ruth's record, Major League Baseball prepared special baseballs with infrared codes on them. These were to be used each time Hank batted. This was to prevent con artists from trying to sell fake baseballs, claiming they were the record-setting ball.

Hank has described the Braves' 1974 spring training as a "nightmare." There were so many reporters there to write about Hank's every movement that he and his teammates could not turn around without bumping into one. Hank wanted to break the record and break it quick. He could not take much more of the pressure and media attention.

The Braves played their first three games of the 1974 season on the road. The Braves were worried that Hank would get his record-tying, and maybe even his record-breaking, homers in another team's ballpark. That would mean that the Braves might miss out on the sold-out crowds they knew would show up to see Hank. The Braves announced that Hank was not going to play in the first three games of the season.

This announcement caught the attention of baseball's commissioner, Bowie Kuhn. Commissioner Kuhn believed that it was in the best interests of baseball for every team to put their best nine players on the field whenever they could. If Hank had been injured or sick, that would have been a different matter. To bench Hank for no reason other than greed, Kuhn thought, was bad for baseball. Therefore, Kuhn ordered that the Braves play Hank in the first three games of the season.

Hank had been waiting all winter to get another hack at Ruth's record, and he did not want to wait any longer. If anyone thought that Hank was going to try anything other than his best to hit home runs during the first three games, they quickly learned they were mistaken.

The Braves first game of the 1974 season was against the Cincinnati Reds at Riverfront Stadium in Cincinnati. On opening day Hank arrived at the ballpark early for a press conference. He announced that he was forming a Hank Aaron Scholarship Fund to help poor kids go to college. Western Union had agreed to donate one dollar to the fund for each telegram of congratulations Hank received when he tied and broke the record.

Then he went out onto the field and played baseball. With his first swing of the season, on April 4, 1974, he smacked home run number 714 off of Reds pitcher Jack Billingham. Hank had looked at Billingham's first four pitches and worked the count to three balls and one strike. The pitch was a sinker, and Hank deposited the ball over the left center-field fence. His eyes misted as he rounded the bases. He was no longer chasing the Babe. He was standing shoulder to shoulder with the greatest baseball player ever. His teammates mobbed him at home plate, then he ran into the stands to give his dad and his wife a hug. Gerald Ford, then the vice president of the United States, walked onto the field to shake Hank's hand.

After the game Hank said he was not able to savor the moment because the Braves had lost the game. Even though he had tied Ruth's record, Hank knew that helping your team win was what the game was all about.

"If we could have won, I would have felt like celebrating. If we had won, I would have popped open the champagne and we would have had a little celebration in the clubhouse. I'll be glad to get all this behind me," Hank said. "I like the exposure, naturally. I'm getting a kick out of it, but I don't like the fact it is overshadowing the performances of such fine players as [teammates] Dusty Baker, Ralph Garr, Dave Johnson, and Darrell Evans. They had fine seasons last year, with some outstanding accomplishments, but nobody seemed to notice."

The pressure of chasing Ruth had affected Hank off the field, but not on it.

"I realized that the only way I can play the game is to do things my way," Hank said after hitting number 714. "I can't get all tense and tight. Fortunately, when I'm on the field, I am able to shut out everything else. And when I'm hitting, I can concentrate fully on the pitcher. I don't know why, that's just the way I've been. When I was in school, my teachers used to comment about how I never got excited. I don't know that I got it from anybody—it's just me."

Hank hit the record-tying home run on the sixth anniversary of the assassination of Dr. Martin Luther King Jr. He was asked after the game if he felt like a hero. He said that King was a hero, but that he (Hank) was just a baseball player.

The Braves played two more games against the Reds in Cincinnati, but Hank did not hit a home run in either of them. The Braves management was relieved that the Braves were coming home and Hank still had not hit number 715.

The Record Is Broken

The first game in Atlanta, the home opener, was played against the Los Angeles Dodgers on April 8. The game was sold out. Standing-room-only tickets were sold. Singing star Pearl Bailey was there to sing the National Anthem and wish Hank her best. Star Sammy Davis Jr. performed before the game. Georgia governor Jimmy Carter, who later became president of the United States, was in the stands.

The stage was set.

In a career filled with spectacular moments, the most spectacular of all came at 9:07 P.M. on April 8, 1974. It was a windy, misty night in Atlanta. A huge national TV audience and 53,775 people in Atlanta Fulton County Stadium were watching.

It was the fourth inning. In the on-deck circle Hank told teammate Darrell Evans, "I'm going to do it right now." At the plate Hank did not swing at the first four pitches, only one of which was in the strike zone. The count was three balls and one strike, just as it had been when Hank hit number 714.

The Dodgers pitcher was Al Downing. Downing threw a slider, low and out over the plate. Forty-year-old Hank Aaron swung with those quick wrists and hit a 385-foot home run over the left-field fence.

At first Hank did not think he had hit the ball well enough to get a homer. But the ball came down in the Braves' bullpen, the area where the Braves' relief pitchers warm up, where it was caught by pitcher Tom House.

Babe Ruth's record, which had stood for 39 years, had been broken.

As Hank rounded the bases, each Dodger infielder congratulated him. Beyond the centerfield fence fireworks went off. Fans began to run onto the field. Hank and his family naturally thought of the death threats Hank had received. Did one of those fans mean to cause Hank harm? As it turned out, they just wanted to pat Hank on the back.

By the time Hank reached home plate his teammates were all there to greet him. After a moment of being mobbed, his teammates cleared a path and Hank's mom threw her arms around him and gave him a big hug. She later said that she hugged him so tightly partly because she was so proud of him, and partly to protect him, in case someone in the crowd wanted to shoot him.

*Hank broke Babe Ruth's home-run record by whacking
number 715 on April 8, 1974.* (National Baseball Hall of Fame
Library, Cooperstown, NY)

Hank's mother hugs her son after his record-breaking home run. Hank later said of the hug, "I didn't know how strong my mother was." (Corbis)

About that hug Hank later said, "I didn't know how strong my mother was."

The fans in Atlanta gave Hank a 10-minute standing ovation. The game stopped and Hank was handed a microphone.

"Thank God it's over," he said to the crowd.

Then something unexpected happened. It started to rain—hard. The ground crew put a tarp over the infield, and the teams retreated to their dugouts for the rain delay.

For a game to be official, it has to go four-and-half innings. If a game is postponed because of rain before that, nothing counts and the game is replayed from the beginning. Had that happened, it would have meant that Hank's 715th home run did not count, and he would have had to break Ruth's record all over again.

But the rain did stop and the game resumed. In the sixth inning, once the home run was officially in the record books, President Richard Nixon, a big baseball fan, called Hank in the Braves dugout to congratulate him. And the Braves went on to win the game.

The Braves had a party for Hank in the clubhouse, and then Hank met the press.

One of the first things Hank did at the postgame press conference was address the rumors that he had not tried as hard as he could during the first three games of the season because he had wanted to break the record in Atlanta.

"I've read stories that I wasn't trying my last game in Cincinnati. I'm not directing this at anyone in particular, but when it is said you're a disgrace on the field, something has to be said.

"I feel now I can relax, my teammates can relax, and that I can go on and have a great year. This is something I wanted. For years, I feel I was slighted by awards and things like that. I worked very hard to get where I am, although I never thought five years ago I would ever be in this position. Now I can consider myself one of the best. Maybe not the best because a lot of great ones have played this game—[Joe] DiMaggio, [Willie] Mays, and Jackie Robinson . . . but I think I can fit in there somewhere.

"The average person doesn't know what a nightmare this has been," Hank continued. "All the same old questions, the controversy . . . I'll enjoy it all a little later."

Telegrams began to arrive, more than 2,000 of them, congratulating Hank for his accomplishment. They came from top athletes from baseball's past as well as other sports. They came from show business stars and from politicians. Hank would read them later.

He was now the home run king. With that title came power—the power to make a difference in the world, just as his mother had dreamed. With the title came responsibility, too.

"I had to set an example for black children, and still do," he later said. "Because they need examples. A white child might need a role model, but a black child needs more than that in this society. He needs hope. People like Jackie Robinson and Jesse Jackson helped me understand that and take it seriously."

After the press conference, tears on his cheeks, he headed home to pray.

Showing His Age

Only two days after Hank hit his 715th home run, the stands at Atlanta Fulton County Stadium were three-quarters empty. With the record broken, it seemed no one was interested in the Braves, or Hank, anymore.

Midway through the season the Braves fired Eddie Mathews as manager, so Hank once again had to say good-bye to his longtime teammate.

In July, the Braves held another Hank Aaron Night. This would turn out to be the last. He received a new Cadillac car. As the season went on, however, Aaron became increasingly unhappy with the Braves—but he was still not ready to retire. Part of him thought he should just up and quit, but another part of him was afraid of retiring. Playing baseball was all he had ever done. He did not know what else there was for him to do.

That year, while the Braves were in New York to play the Mets, Hank rode in a parade through Harlem, an African American neighborhood in Manhattan. He had an opportunity to meet the widows of former New York Yankee sluggers Babe Ruth and Lou Gehrig. He also had a chance to speak to a crowd, many of whom were young-sters. Hank recalled his own youth, listening to Jackie Robinson speak about never giving up on a dream. Hank tried to inspire those kids just the way Robinson had inspired him years before.

The 1974 season was Hank's worst ever. His age was starting to show. His body hurt and he had trouble getting himself inspired to play hard. He had only 340 at-bats in

1974, playing a little more than half the time. He hit .268, hit only 20 home runs, and knocked in only 69 runs. For the last game of the season in Atlanta, attendance was only 11,000. The stadium looked empty.

Hank hit his final home run as a Brave during that last game. Hank said, "I circled the bases one last time, stepped on home plate, ran to the dugout and kept right on going to the clubhouse. . . . I was too choked up to face the crowd. I needed to be alone. The Braves had been my life for 21 years."

The Braves won more than they lost that year. They had a record of 88 wins and 74 losses, but finished 13 games behind the division-winning Dodgers.

Traded

During the off-season between 1974 and 1975 Hank traveled to Japan, where baseball is just as popular as it is in the United States. He quickly learned that he was a hero there. At the airport 2,000 reporters were on hand to greet the new American home run king.

There were 50,000 people in the stands of the Japanese ballpark when Hank and the Japanese home-run king, Sadaharu Oh, had a home-run hitting contest—not unlike the one on the *Home Run Derby* TV show that Hank had starred on in the 1950s. Aaron defeated Oh, 10 home runs to nine.

It was while he was in Japan that Hank learned he had been traded to the Milwaukee Brewers, who then played in the American League. (Milwaukee, after four years of not having Major League Baseball, received an expansion franchise, the Brewers, in 1970.) This was very good news as far as Hank was concerned.Milwaukee was his favorite city—and he knew the people of Milwaukee felt the same way about him.

Hank was to finish his big-league career in the same city where he started, but with a different team. (Coincidentally, this was also true of the other two top career home-run hitters at the time. Babe Ruth began his major league career with the Boston Red Sox and finished with the Boston Braves. Willie Mays began his career with the New York Giants and finished with the New York Mets.)

Back in Milwaukee

On opening day in Milwaukee the stands were packed. With Hank in the lineup, the Brewers drew a record crowd for their first game. Hank was emotional as he made his Brewers debut. He had a base hit and an RBI in that first game. A few days later he hit his first home run as a Brewer. In the third week of the season Hank broke another of Babe Ruth's records, this one for career RBIs.

Hank, now too old and slow to play in the field, was assigned to be the Brewers' designated hitter. (In the National League pitchers hit for themselves. In the American League designated hitters bat in the pitcher's spot.) When he wasn't hitting, Hank spent much of his time teaching his teammates about the game.

Teammate George Scott later said, "I had the best season of my career that year, and I believe it was because of Hank Aaron."

It was not a good year for Hank though. His numbers fell off even further from the previous year's lows. In 1975 his batting average was a poor .234. He managed only 12 home runs.

Hank made excuses for his poor performance, none of which involved his age. He told himself that, being a designated hitter, he could not concentrate the way he had when he played in the outfield. He told himself that he was unfamiliar with the pitchers in the American League and that was why hitting was suddenly so difficult. But the truth was, he was getting old. It happens to all ballplayers sooner or later.

In 1975 yet another color line was broken. Frank Robinson, the superstar of the 1960s who played for the Cincinnati Reds and the Baltimore Orioles, became baseball's first African American manager, taking the helm for the Cleveland Indians.

Last Year

Hank played one more year. His ability to hit did not improve. Signs that he was growing older were everywhere. He now needed to wear glasses to read. He hit only .229 and added 10 home runs to his record total. Five of those homers came in a single weeklong hot streak in June. Hank's biggest home run of the year came in July when he hit one in extra innings to defeat the Texas Rangers. It was the second-to-last home run of his career.

Hank hit his final home run on July 20, 1976, against pitcher Dick Drago of the California Angels. It was number 755 of his career—baseball's new magic number.

At the beginning of September, Hank was walking up the steps of the Brewers' dugout when his bad knee buckled under him. The next day had already been scheduled as Hank Aaron Day in Milwaukee, and Hank used the ceremony to officially announce his retirement. He played only a few more games after that, including the last game of the season, which the Brewers played against the Tigers in Detroit.

In his final at-bat, Hank had an infield single that knocked in a run. He ended his career playing in 3,298 games, with 12,364 at-bats, and knocking in 2,297 runs. All of those numbers are all-time records unlikely to be broken soon. He left the game as a pinch runner replaced him, and he smiled all the way to the dugout.

Hank takes a swing during his final game, October 4, 1976.
(Associated Press)

In addition to being Hank's last year as a ballplayer, 1976 was also Ted Turner's first year as the owner of Hank's old team, the Braves. Turner was a millionaire who helped develop cable television and owned both Superstation TBS and the all-news station CNN.

"Ted Turner was the best thing that could have happened to me," Hank said.

As the new owner of the Braves, one of Turner's first moves was to offer Hank Aaron a job.

6

LIFE OFF THE FIELD

Even when Hank's baseball playing days were over, he still managed to break color lines. He became the first African American to work in the front office for a big-league team. He went back to work for the Braves, this time wearing a suit and tie.

He started out as the Braves' director of player development. In that position he helped decide which new ballplayers the Braves would sign. Once they were signed, he worked with the young players to help determine which ones would be promoted toward the major league club. One of his first moves was to hire his brother Tommie to manage the Braves' top farm club in Richmond, Virginia.

Hank enjoyed the move back to Atlanta. He later said, "There is no other black community in the world like Atlanta's, and Billye thrived in it. Plus, moving back to Atlanta meant I would get to see my children more."

Billye and Hank Aaron wave to the crowds in Atlanta on the 25th anniversary of Hank's 715th home run. (Associated Press)

Before Hank joined the front office, the Braves were one of the worst teams in the National League. Soon after he was hired, they became one of the best, and they have remained one of the best ever since.

Cooperstown

Official rules say that a baseball player has to wait five years after retirement before he can be inducted into the Baseball Hall of Fame in Cooperstown, New York. So, in

1982 in his first year of eligibility, Hank Aaron was voted into the Hall of Fame. He received 97.8 percent of the vote, the second highest percentage of any ballplayer.

Hank was elected into the Hall the same year as Frank Robinson, another African American pioneer. Robinson had slugged more than 500 home runs himself and had gone on to become the first black baseball manager.

During his short induction speech in Cooperstown, Hank said, "It has been a long and winding road." He thanked Jackie Robinson for paving the way for African American ballplayers and said, "A man's ability is only limited by his opportunity."

Also in 1982 a statue of Hank was erected on the plaza in front of Atlanta Fulton County Stadium. When the Braves moved to a new ballpark, Turner Field, the statue moved along with them.

That same year was also touched by sadness. Hank's brother Tommie was diagnosed with a blood disease called leukemia. Two years later Tommie died of the disease. Hank was at his brother's bedside when he died and later called it "the hardest night of my life."

Vice President

In 1990 Hank was promoted to senior vice president of the Braves. He works closely with the team president and general manager and has a lot of input into any trades the

Braves make. Hank said he would do anything he could to help the Braves, except for one thing. "If I go to their games," he said, "I can't sit in the stands. I'd either have to make people mad by not signing autographs, or I'd be interrupted constantly. So, I'd rather watch at home."

He is also a member of the board of directors for both the Braves and Ted Turner's station WTBS, which broadcasts all of the Braves' games.

Humanitarian and Legend

Hank first became involved in charity work while still an active ballplayer. He set up the Hank Aaron Scholarship Fund to help underprivileged kids go to college. In 1995 the organization changed its name to the Chasing the Dream Foundation, after the TBS documentary about Aaron that was nominated for an Academy Award for Best Documentary Film. Forty-four deserving kids receive a scholarship every year. Hank hopes one day to make that 755 kids a year, one for each home run he hit during his career.

Aaron also teamed up with Sadaharu Oh, the Japanese home run king, to help popularize baseball throughout the world. He also serves on the executive board for PUSH (People United to Save Humanity) and the NAACP (National Association for the Advancement of Colored People). Ever since Tommie's death in 1984, Hank has

(Landov)

been active in fund-raising for cancer and leukemia research.

In 1999 Major League Baseball introduced the annual Hank Aaron Award, which is given to the best all-around hitter in each league.

Except for an occasional game of catch with one of his grandchildren, Hank never plays baseball anymore. But his record-breaking career is one that fans will not soon forget. In a 1990 poll, fans were asked to name the most memorable moment in baseball history. The winner: Hank Aaron's 715th home run, hit in 1974.

TIME LINE

1934 Henry "Hank" Aaron born to Estella and Herbert Aaron on February 5 in Mobile, Alabama

1947 Jackie Robinson breaks color line by becoming first African American to play Major League Baseball since the 19th century

1951 Plays shortstop for the semipro team, the Mobile Black Bears, for $10 per game

1952 Leaves Mobile for the first time to play professional baseball for the Indianapolis Clowns of the Negro American League; plays on an integrated team for the first time—a farm team of the Milwaukee Braves in Eau Claire, Wisconsin

1953 Promoted to the Jacksonville Tars of the Sally League during the first year that league is integrated; marries Barbara Lucas of Jacksonville;

spends honeymoon in Puerto Rico and plays Winter
League baseball there

1954   Promoted to the major league Milwaukee Braves
and becomes the team's left fielder; hits first major
league home run on April 23

1956   Wins National League batting title with average of
.326

1957   Wins National League Most Valuable Player Award;
Braves win world championship

1966   Braves move to Atlanta

1968   Hits 500th career home run and wins fourth
National League home run title

1970   Makes 3,000th career hit on May 17

1971   Hits 600th career home run on April 27; divorce
from Barbara becomes final

1973   On July 21 becomes second player ever to hit 700
home runs; marries Billye Williams, an Atlanta talk-
show host

1974   On April 4 ties Babe Ruth's record of 714 home
runs; hits 715th home run on April 8, setting new
world record; traded to the Milwaukee Brewers,
then of the American League

1976 Hits final home run of career, number 755, on July
20; retires from baseball; hired as an executive for
the Atlanta Braves, becoming the first African
American to work in the front office of a major
league team

1982 Inducted into the Baseball Hall of Fame in Cooperstown, New York, on August 1

1990 Poll taken of baseball fans determines Hank's 715th
home run to be baseball history's most memorable
moment

HOW TO BECOME A PROFESSIONAL ATHLETE

THE JOB

Unlike amateur athletes who play or compete in amateur circles for titles or trophies only, professional athletic teams compete against one another to win titles, championships, and series; team members are paid salaries and bonuses for their work.

The athletic performances of individual teams are evaluated according to the nature and rules of each specific sport: Usually the winning team compiles the highest score, as in football, basketball, and soccer. Competitions are organized by local, regional, national, and international organizations and associations, whose primary functions are to promote the sport and sponsor competitive events. Within a professional sport there are usually different levels of competition based on age, ability, and gender. There are often different designations and divisions within one sport. Professional baseball, for example, is made up of the two major leagues (American and National) each made up of three divisions, East, Central, and West, and the minor leagues (Single-A, Double-A, Triple-A). All of these teams are considered professional because the players are compensated for their work, but the financial rewards are the greatest in the major leagues.

Whatever the team sport, most team members specialize in a specific area of the game. In gymnastics, for example, the entire six-member team trains on all of the gymnastic apparatuses—balance beam, uneven bars, vault, and floor exercise—but usually each of the six gymnasts excels in only one or two areas. Those gymnasts who do excel in all four events are likely to do well in the individual, all-around title, which is a part of the team competition. Team members in football, basketball, baseball, soccer, and hockey all assume different positions, some of which change depending on whether or not the team is trying to score a goal (offensive positions) or prevent the opposition from scoring one (defensive positions). During team practices, athletes focus on their specific role in a game, whether that is defensive, offensive, or both. For example, a pitcher will spend some time running bases and throwing to other positions, but the majority of his or her time will most likely be spent practicing pitching.

Professional teams train for most of the year, but unlike athletes in individual sports, the athletes who are members of a team usually have more of an off-season. Professional athletes' training programs differ according to the season. Following an off-season, most team sports have a training season in which they begin to increase the intensity of their workouts after a period of relative inactivity, in order to develop or maintain strength, cardiovascular ability, flexibility, endurance, speed, and quickness, as well as to focus on technique and control. During the season the team coach, physician, trainers, and physical therapists organize specific routines, programs, or exercises to target game skills as well as individual athletic weaknesses, whether skill-related or from injury.

These workouts also vary according to the difficulty of the game schedule. During a playoff or championship series, the coach and athletic staff realize that a rigorous workout in between games might tax the athletes' strength, stamina, or even mental preparedness, jeopardizing the outcome of the next game. Instead, the coach might prescribe a mild workout followed by intensive stretching. In addition to stretching and exercising the specific muscles used in any given sport, athletes concentrate on developing excellent eating and sleeping habits that will help them remain in top condition throughout the year. Abstaining from drinking alcoholic beverages during a season is a practice to which many professional athletes adhere.

The coaching or training staff often films the games and practices so that the team can benefit from watching their individual exploits, as well as its combined play. By watching their performances, team members can learn how to improve their techniques and strategies. It is common for professional teams to also study other teams' moves and strategies in order to determine a method of coping with the other teams' plays during a game.

REQUIREMENTS

High School

Most professional athletes demonstrate tremendous skill and interest in their sport well before high school. High school offers student athletes the opportunity to gain experience in the field in a structured and competitive environment. Under the guidance of a coach, you can begin developing suitable training programs and learn about health, nutrition, and conditioning issues.

High school also offers you the opportunity to experiment with a variety of sports and a variety of positions within a sport. Most junior varsity and some varsity high school teams allow you to try out different positions and begin to discover whether you have more of an aptitude for the defensive dives of a goalie or for the forwards' front-line action. High school coaches will help you learn to expand upon your strengths and abilities and develop yourself more fully as an athlete. High school is also an excellent time to begin developing the concentration powers, leadership skills, and good sportsmanship necessary for success on the field.

People who hope to become professional athletes should take a full load of high school courses including four years of English, math, and science, as well as health and physical education. A solid high school education will help ensure success in college (often the next step in becoming a professional athlete) and may help you earn a college athletic scholarship. A high school diploma will certainly give you something to fall back on if an injury, a change in career goals, or other circumstance prevents you from earning a living as an athlete.

Postsecondary Training

College is important for future professional athletes for several reasons. It provides the opportunity to gain skill and strength in your sport before you try to succeed in the pros, and it also offers you the chance of being observed by professional scouts.

Perhaps most important, a college education provides you with a valuable degree that you can use if you do not earn a living as a professional athlete or after your professional career ends. College athletes major in everything from communications to premed and enjoy careers as coaches, broadcasters, teachers, doctors, actors, and businesspeople, to name a few. As with high school sports, college athletes must maintain certain academic standards in order to be permitted to compete in intercollegiate play.

Other Requirements

If you want to be a professional athlete, you must be fully committed to succeeding. You must work almost nonstop to improve your conditioning and skills, and not give up when you do not succeed as quickly or as easily as you had hoped. And even then, because the competition is so fierce, the goal of earning a living as a professional athlete is still difficult to reach. For this reason, professional athletes must not get discouraged easily. They must have the self-confidence and ambition to keep working and keep trying. Professional athletes also must have a love for their sport that compels them to want to reach their fullest potential.

EXPLORING

Students interested in pursuing a career in professional sports should start playing that sport as much and as early as possible. Most junior high and high schools have well-established programs in the sports that are played at the professional level.

If a team sport does not exist in your school that does not mean your chances of playing it have evaporated. Petition your school board to establish it as a school sport and set aside funds for it. In the meantime organize other students into a club team, scheduling practices and unofficial games. If the sport is a recognized team sport in the United States or Canada, contact the sport's professional organization for additional information; if anyone would have helpful tips for gaining recognition, the professional organization would. Also, try calling the local or state athletic board to see whether or not any other schools in your area recognize it as a team sport, and make a list of those teams and try scheduling exhibition games with them. Your goal is to show your school or school board that other students have a definite interest in the game and that other schools recognize it.

To determine if you really want to commit to pursuing a professional career in your team sport, talk to coaches, trainers, and any athletes who are currently pursuing a professional career. You can also contact professional organizations and associations for information on how to best prepare for a career in their sport. Sometimes there are specialized training programs available, and the best way to find out is to get in contact with the people whose job it is to promote the sport.

EMPLOYERS

Professional athletes are employed by private and public ownership groups throughout the United States and Canada. At the highest male professional level, there are 32 National Football League franchises, 30 Major League Baseball franchises, 29 National Basketball Association franchises, 30 National Hockey League franchises, and 10 Major League Soccer franchises. The Women's National Basketball Association has 16 franchises.

STARTING OUT

Most team sports have some official manner of establishing which teams acquire which players, often this is referred to as a draft, although sometimes members of a professional team are chosen through a competition. Usually the draft occurs between the college and professional levels of the sport. The National Basketball Association (NBA), for example, has its NBA College Draft. During the draft the owners and managers of professional basketball teams choose players in an order based on the team's performance in the previous season. This means that the team with the worst record in the previous season has a greater chance of getting to choose first from the list of available players.

Furthermore, professional athletes must meet the requirements established by the organizing bodies of their respective sport. Sometimes this means meeting a physical requirement, such as age, height, and weight; sometimes it means fulfilling a number of required stunts, or participating in a certain number of competitions. Professional organizations usually arrange it so that athlctes can build up their skills and level of play by participating in lower-level competitions. College sports, as mentioned before, are an excellent way to improve one's skills while pursuing an education.

ADVANCEMENT

Professional athletes in team sports advance in three ways: when their team advances, when they are traded to better teams, and when they negotiate better contracts. In all three instances, the individual team member who works and practices hard, and who gives his or her best performance in game after game, achieves this. Winning teams also receive a deluge of media attention that often creates celebrities out of individual players, which in turn provides these top players with opportunities for financially rewarding commercial endorsements.

Professional athletes are usually represented by *sports agents* in the behind-the-scenes deals that determine for which teams they will be playing and what they will be paid. These agents may also be involved with other key decisions involving commercial endorsements, personal income taxes, and financial investments of the athlete's revenues.

In the moves from high school athletics to collegiate athletics and from collegiate athletics to the pros, coaches and scouts are continually scouring the ranks of high school and college teams for new talent; they're most interested in the athletes who consistently deliver points or prevent the opposition from scoring. There is simply no substitute for success.

A college education, however, can prepare all athletes for the day when their bodies can no longer compete at the top level, whether because of age or an unforeseen injury. Every athlete should be prepared to move into another career, whether it is related to the world of sports or not.

Professional athletes do have other options, especially those who have graduated from a four-year college or university. Many go into some area of coaching, sports administration, management, or broadcasting. The professional athlete's unique insight and perspective can be a real asset in these careers. Other athletes simultaneously pursue other interests, some completely unrelated to their sport, such as education, business, social welfare, or the arts. Many continue to stay involved with the sport they have loved since childhood, coaching young children or volunteering with local school teams.

EARNINGS

Today professional athletes who are members of top-level teams earn hundreds of thousands of dollars in prize money at professional competitions; the top players or athletes in each sport earn as much or more in endorsements and advertising, usually for sports-related products and services, but increasingly for products or services completely unrelated to their sport. Such salaries and other incomes are not representative of the whole field of professional athletes, but are only indicative of the fantastic revenues a few rare athletes with extraordinary talent can hope to earn. In 2002 athletes had median annual earnings of $45,320, according to the U.S. Department of Labor. Ten percent earned less than $14,090.

Perhaps the only caveat to the financial success of an elite athlete is the individual's character or personality. An athlete with a bad temper or who is prone to unsportsmanlike behavior may still be able to participate in team play, helping to win games and garner trophies, but he or she won't necessarily be able to cash in on the commercial endorsements. Advertisers are notoriously fickle about the spokespeople they choose to endorse products; some athletes have lost million-dollar accounts because of their bad behavior on and off the court.

WORK ENVIRONMENT

Athletes compete in many different conditions, according to the setting of the sport (indoors or outdoors) and the rules of the organizing or governing bodies. Athletes who participate in football or soccer, for example, often compete in hot, rainy, or freezing conditions, but at any point, organizing officials can call off the match, or postpone competition until the weather improves.

Indoor events are less subject to cancellation. However, since it is in the best interests of an organization not to risk the athletes' health, any condition that might adversely affect the outcome of a competition is usually reason to cancel or postpone it. The coach or team physician, on the other hand, may withdraw an athlete from a game if that athlete is injured or ill. Nerves and fear are not good reasons to default on a competition, and part of ascending into the ranks of professional athletes means learning to cope with the anxiety that comes with competition. Some athletes, however, actually thrive on the nervous tension.

In order to reach the elite level of any sport, athletes must begin their careers early. Most professional athletes have been honing their skills since they were quite young. Athletes fit hours of practice time into an already full day; many famous players practiced on their own before school, as well as for several hours after school during team practice. Competitions are often far from the young athlete's home, which means they must travel on a bus or in a van with the team and coaching staff. Sometimes young athletes are placed in special training programs far from their homes and parents. They live with other athletes training for the same sport or on the same team, and only see their parents for holidays and vacations. The separation from a child's parents and family can be difficult; often an athlete's family decides to move in order to be closer to the child's training facility.

The expenses of a sport can be overwhelming, as is the time an athlete must devote to practice and travel to and from competitions. Although most high school athletic programs pay for many expenses, if the athlete wants additional training or private coaching, the child's parents must come up with the extra money. Sometimes young athletes can get official sponsors or they might qualify for an athletic scholarship from the training program. In addition to specialized equipment and clothing, the athlete must sometimes pay for a coach, travel expenses, competition fees, and, depending on the sport, time at the facility or gym where he or she practices. Gymnasts, for example, train for years as individuals, and then compete for positions on national or international teams. Up until the time they are accepted (and usually during their participation in the team), these gymnasts must pay for their expenses—from coach to travel to uniforms to room and board away from home.

Even with the years of hard work, practice, and financial sacrifice that most athletes and their families must endure, there is no guarantee that an athlete will achieve the rarest of the rare in the sports world—financial reward. An athlete needs to truly love the sport at which he or she excels, and also have a nearly insatiable ambition and work ethic.

OUTLOOK

The outlook for professional athletes will vary depending on the sport, its popularity, and the number of positions open with professional teams. On the whole, the outlook for the field of professional sports is healthy, but the number of jobs will not increase dramatically. Some sports, however, may experience a rise in popularity, which may translate into greater opportunities for higher salaries, prize monies, and commercial endorsements.

TO LEARN MORE ABOUT PROFESSIONAL ATHLETES

BOOKS

Coffey, Wayne. *Carl Lewis: The Triumph of Discipline.* Woodbridge, Conn.: Blackbirch Press, 1992.

Freedman, Russell. *Babe Didrikson Zaharias.* New York: Clarion, 1999.

Krull, Kathleen. *Lives of the Athletes: Thrills, Spills (And What the Neighbors Thought).* New York: Harcourt Brace, 1997.

Rudeen, Kenneth. *Jackie Robinson.* New York: HarperTrophy, 1996.

Stewart, Mark. *Tiger Woods: Driving Force.* Danbury, Conn.: Children's Press, 1998.

Updyke, Rosemary Kissinger. *Jim Thorpe, the Legend Remembered*. New York: Pelican, 1997.

WEBSITES AND ORGANIZATIONS

Young people who are interested in becoming professional athletes should contact the professional organizations for the sport in which they would like to compete, such as the National Hockey League, U.S. Tennis Association, the Professional Golfer's Association, or the National Bowling Association. Ask for information on requirements, training centers, coaches, and so on.

For a free brochure and information on the Junior Olympics and more, write to

Amateur Athletic Union
c/o The Walt Disney World Resort
P.O. Box 10000
Lake Buena Vista, FL 32830-1000
http://www.aausports.org

For additional information on athletics
American Alliance for Health, Physical Education, Recreation, and Dance
1900 Association Drive
Reston, VA 20191
http://www.aahperd.org

The popular magazine *Sports Illustrated for Kids* also has a website.

Sports Illustrated for Kids

http://www.sikids.com

Visit the U.S. Olympic Committee's website for the latest sporting news and information about upcoming Olympic competitions.

United States Olympic Committee

http://www.olympic-usa.org

The following website provides information about and links to women in all kinds of sports:

Women in Sports

http://www.makeithappen.com/wis/index.html

TO LEARN MORE ABOUT HANK AARON AND BASEBALL

BOOKS

Aaron, Hank. *Aaron*. New York: Ty Crowell Co., 1974.

Aaron, Henry. *Hitting the Aaron Way*. Upper Saddle River, New Jersey: Prentice Hall, 1974.

Benson, Michael. *Ballparks of North America*. Jefferson, North Carolina: 1989.

Burchard, Marshall. *Sports Hero: Henry Aaron*. New York: Putnam, 1974.

Golenbock, Peter. *Hank Aaron: Brave in Every Way.* New York: Harcourt, 2001.

Hahn, James, Lynn Hahn, and Howard Schroeder. *Henry!: The Sports Career of Henry Aaron.* New York: Crestwood House, 1981.

Levanthal, Josh. *The World Series.* New York: Black Dog & Leventhal Publishers, 2001.

Plimpton, George. *One for the Record: The Inside Story of Hank Aaron's Chase for the Home Run Record.* New York: HarperCollins, 1974.

Poling, Jerry and Allen H. Selig. *A Summer Up North: Henry Aaron and the Legend of Eau Claire Baseball.* Madison, Wis.: University of Wisconsin Press, 2002.

Spencer, Lauren. *Hank Aaron.* New York: Rosen Publishing Group, 2003.

Sullivan, George. *Hank Aaron.* New York: Putnam, 1975.

Sweet, Kimberly. *Hank Aaron: The Life of the Home Run King.* Montgomery, Ala.: New South, Inc., 2002.

MAGAZINES

Benson, Michael, "Aaron's 715th Baseball's Most Memorable Moment," *All-Time Baseball Greats*, (September 1990): 27.

WEBSITES AND ORGANIZATIONS

Larry Schwartz. "Henry Aaron: Hammerin' Back at Racism," ESPN.com. Available online. URL: http://

espn.go.com/sportscentury/features/00006764.html. Accessed January 16, 2004.

The Sporting News. "Hank Aaron Scrapbook." Available online. URL: http://www.sportingnews.com/archives/aaron/. Accessed January 16, 2004.

National Baseball Hall of Fame and Museum
25 Main Street
P.O. Box 590
Cooperstown, NY 13326
(607) 547-7200
http://www.baseballhalloffame.org

BASEBALL GLOSSARY

ball any pitch that fails to go through the strike zone

barnstorming traveling from town to town, informally and not as part of a league schedule

double play any play that results in two outs, most commonly a ground ball struck with a man on first base; a throw to a fielder touching second base forces the runner out and a second throw to first base gets the batter out

ground ball a batted ball that bounces along the ground

MVP Most Valuable Player

pennant league championship

pitchers' duel a low-scoring game

popped out a batted ball that goes almost straight up in the air and is usually easily caught for an out by a player in the field

relay throw   if an outfielder fields the ball far enough from the infield, it may take more than one throw to get the ball to its desired destination, usually one of the bases or home plate; the player who fields the ball, in this case, throws the ball to the "relay" man, who executes a relay throw to the desired base; or, the second throw in an infield double play

shut out   to complete a game without allowing the opponent to score

sinker   a pitch that breaks sharply downward near home plate, usually causing the batter to swing over it

slugging average   A statistic designed to measure a batter's ability to hit with power. It is the total number of bases a batter has gained through his hits, divided by his number of times at bat. A single is worth one base, a double worth two bases, a triple worth three, and a home run worth four. A batter who homers every fourth at-bat and otherwise gets no hits has the same slugging average as a batter who hits a single every at-bat: 1.000.

spitball   ball made slippery with saliva or other substance by a pitcher, in order to make it curve suddenly when thrown

strike zone   area over home plate between the top of the batter's knees and his armpits

Triple Crown   to lead the league in batting average,
   home runs, and runs batted in

walk   play in which the batter is awarded first base
   because the pitcher has thrown four pitches out of the
   strike zone; also known as "base on balls"

INDEX

Page numbers in *italics* indicate illustrations.

ABOUT THE AUTHOR

Michael Benson has written biographies of Ronald Reagan, Bill Clinton, William Howard Taft, Malcolm X, Muhammad Ali, Lance Armstrong, Wayne Gretzky, Dale Earnhardt, and Gloria Estefan. He is the former editor of *All-Time Baseball Greats, Fight Game,* and *Stock Car Spectacular* magazines. He is the author of more than 30 books, including *The Encyclopedia of the JFK Assassination* and *Complete Idiot's Guides to NASA, The CIA, National Security, Aircraft Carriers, Submarines,* and *Modern China.* Originally from Rochester, New York, he is a graduate of Hofstra University. He enjoys his life with his wife and two children in Brooklyn, New York, and his goal is to one day write the Great American Novel. He dedicates this work to R.A.H.L.S.